Books may be ordered through booksellers or by contacting:

Wainwright Global
www.WainwrightGlobal.com
1 (800) 711-4346

Because of the dynamic nature of the Internet, any web addresses or links contained in this book may have changed since publication and may no longer be valid. The views expressed in this work are solely those of the author and do not necessarily reflect the views of the publisher, and the publisher hereby disclaims any responsibility for them.

The author of this book does not dispense medical advice or prescribe the use of any technique as a form of treatment for physical, emotional, or medical problems without the advice of a physician, either directly or indirectly. The intent of the author is only to offer information of a general nature to help you in your quest for becoming a better person. In the event you use any of the information in this book for yourself, which is your constitutional right, the author and the publisher assume no responsibility for your actions.

Print information available on the last page.

ISBN: 979-8-9912217-6-4 (sc)
ISBN: 979-8-9912217-7-1 (hc)
ISBN: 979-8-9912217-8-8 (e)

Library of Congress Pre-Assigned Control Number: 1-15021912861
Library of Congress Registration Number: TXu 2-528-326

Wainwright Global rev. date: 03/03/2026

Awakening to Divine Purpose

A GUIDE THROUGH THE SIX STAGES
OF SPIRITUAL TRANSFORMATION

By: Barbara G. Wainwright

About Barbara G. Wainwright

~ Table of Contents ~

Acknowledgements

This book would not have been possible without the encouragement and support of my loved ones: my husband, Heath Chadwick; my daughter, Dallas James; my artist in the Philippines, Reigel Allen Munsayac; my photographer, Eric Quiros (my photo); Keith Brockway (cover photo) and the many coaches who, during our classes, inspired me to step up, persevere, and bring this work to completion.

I want to acknowledge Keith Brockway as he shared a photo with me that was the inspiration for me to complete this book and his encouragement for me to continue writing moved me into action. Keith captured the cover photo in Fort Wayne, Indiana.

Gilda Simonet is my co-host on "The Power of Now: A guide to Spiritual Enlightenment with Gilda and Barbara" and has continued to "Show Up for God" and me. She is a true blessing in my life.

Dedication

I dedicate this book to all who are seeking hope, guidance, and enlightenment through their own connection to the Divine. May you find within these pages words that are heartfelt, uplifting, and deeply encouraging—embodying wisdom, lived experience, and spiritual insight. I love you.

Introduction

Change is inevitable in life. You can either resist it and risk being run over by it, or you can choose to cooperate with it, adapt to it, and learn how to benefit from it. When you embrace change, you begin to see it as an opportunity for growth.

Awakening to Divine Purpose: A Guide Through the Six Stages of Spiritual Transformation is a powerful and insightful guide for anyone navigating life's inevitable changes and seeking genuine transformation. The spiritual journey often begins with dissatisfaction—the quiet realization that "something is missing"—or through overwhelming devastation, what many call "the dark night of the soul." Yet, it is within these moments that awakening takes root. What once seemed like suffering often becomes the very turning point that lifts us out of darkness and into light.

What makes the journey to awakening so profound is the focus on personal responsibility and inner power. Our thoughts create our reality. Learning to become conscious observers of our thinking patterns—and mastering them through self-discipline—is the beginning of self-control. When we align our conscious desires with our subconscious beliefs, life begins to flow with ease. Resistance, in many cases, is simply a sign that subconscious programming is working against our true path. Through repetition, emotional intelligence, and conscious awareness, we can reprogram our inner landscape and open the door to breakthrough and renewal of our Divine Purpose.

The stages outlined in this book move you from searching for answers outside yourself to discovering that the answers have been within you all along. Your deep inner guidance—your intuition—serves as a spiritual compass, pointing you back toward truth. Along the way, you learn to live by principles such as honesty, integrity, and acceptance, recognizing that accountability to yourself is essential for your spiritual growth.

Ultimately, the journey to enlightenment culminates in surrender—turning our will over to God and discovering our Divine Purpose. Each of us is born with unique, divinely inspired gifts meant to be shared with the world. When doubt, fear, or indecision—the "Unholy Trio," as Napoleon Hill called them—arises, we are invited to move forward anyway, trusting the call within.

The final stage—Sharing Newfound Beliefs and Divine Gifts—is both the reward and the calling. When we step outside our comfort zone and act in alignment with our Divine Purpose, the Universe conspires on our behalf. Miracles unfold. Opportunities arise. We become instruments of grace.

The message woven throughout these pages is simple yet profound: show up for God, and God will show up for you in miraculous ways.

If you are ready to stop playing small and embrace the extraordinary life you were meant to live, this book will guide you toward that transformation. Boldness, as W. H. Murray said, "has genius, power, and magic in it."

I believe there are definitive stages to a spiritual awakening. It rarely happens overnight, though there are always exceptions to the rule. Two individuals who immediately come to mind are Eckhart Tolle and Bill Wilson. Each experienced a spontaneous awakening, though both endured deep suffering before their moment of enlightenment.

For most of us, however, the path is longer—marked by turmoil, questions, wonder, and awe—as we gradually weave our way toward serenity and acceptance of "what is." With these thoughts in mind, I invite you to join me in exploring the six stages of spiritual awakening as I have come to know them. My hope is that, as you read, you will recognize pieces of your own story within these stages and find encouragement, clarity, and inspiration for your spiritual journey ahead.

STAGE 1

Awakening:
Becoming Conscious

Triggers ~ The Catalysts for Change

There is usually a trigger—some event that sets us on a spiritual quest, a search for the meaning of life. These experiences vary, but they all serve as catalysts for awakening. As the saying goes, *It takes what it takes*. In this context, it means the universe conspires on our behalf to create the circumstances that lead us toward our highest good.

At the time, what we face may not seem like a catalyst for transformation. Yet, in hindsight, we often see that those very challenges were the turning points that lifted us out of darkness and into the light.

Dissatisfaction ~ Something is Missing

At some point in life, dissatisfaction begins to stir. You may catch yourself wondering, *Is this all there is?* A low level of discontent has settled in and it's not going away; in fact, it is growing.

By the world's standards, you should be happy. You have the house with the white picket fence, the marriage, the job, the two or three kids, the car in the driveway, maybe even the boat and the framed degrees on the wall. You've gathered the pieces that are supposed to add up to fulfillment. You now have everything you ever thought you wanted.

And yet you realize that something is missing.

You worked so hard to get here, only to realize that "here" feels strangely empty.

The happiness you expected doesn't arrive. You come to see that the relationships, the money, the possessions, and the status symbols—while nice—don't fill the deeper longing inside you. You notice an unsettling restlessness, a yearning for a deeper connection.

This is often the first stage of awakening: dissatisfaction. It is not failure. It is not a flaw.

It is the whisper of your soul, reminding you that you were made for more.

Devastation ~ The Dark Night of the Soul

"God, grant me the serenity to accept the things I cannot change, the courage to change the things I can, and the wisdom to know the difference."

~ Reinhold Niebuhr

Perhaps you have experienced a deep loss and found that the world, as you once knew it, has ceased to exist. Life begins to feel meaningless, and the emptiness seems overwhelming. You may wonder why you are still here and how you can possibly go on. This experience has often been called "the dark night of the soul." It is not uncommon, during an awakening, to experience a profound reality shift—where nothing makes sense and things that once seemed important suddenly feel trivial.

What we can develop is the ability to control our own thoughts and actions. What we *cannot* control are the thoughts or actions of others. It is important to recognize that we alone are responsible for our own way of being. If you find yourself in a situation where you are not loved, appreciated, or honored, you carry the responsibility to take action on your own behalf and remove yourself from that environment.

The way we respond to others—whether they attack us or offer us praise—is always our responsibility. If you are triggered by someone's words or actions, it is essential to recognize that the trigger lies within you. It is not the other person's responsibility to resolve it. That individual has entered your life as a catalyst for growth, helping you uncover blocked energy and offering you the opportunity to release and heal.

Navigating Life's Chaos

"I have so much chaos in my life, it's become normal. You become used to it. You have to just relax, calm down, take a deep breath and try to see how you can make things work rather than complain about how they're wrong."

~ Tom Welling

"In a quiet place, close your eyes, take a deep breath, and go inward. Place your attention on your heart, in the center of your chest. Sit quietly and easily let your attention remain there."

~ Deepak Chopra

Sometimes, especially when we are beginning our spiritual quest, life throws us curveballs. The best way to handle these situations is to navigate life's chaos with a calm perspective and a problem-solving attitude. It is essential to find a peaceful moment amidst the turbulence. There are many ways to return to the present moment, and doing so helps you center yourself, reducing stress and anxiety. When life feels overwhelming, try to locate a quiet space, seek solitude, or take a short walk.

You can easily shift your energy into a state of peace by closing your eyes and taking several deep breaths. As you breathe slowly in and out, focus all your attention on your heart. With another deep breath, allow yourself to connect with the present moment. With each inhale and exhale, feel the muscles from your head to your toes begin to relax. Notice an inner calm enveloping you, as a sense of unity with everything around you grows. Then direct your attention toward the areas of your body where you are holding tension. Sending thoughts of love and positivity to those areas can help dissipate the tightness, often within a brief period. This practice ultimately shifts your energy and mindset, enabling you to address challenges with a calm, proactive perspective.

By caring for yourself in this way, you are better equipped to approach challenges with empathy and compassion. Remember to nurture your own well-being so that you can shine brightly and guide others with your light. As you show up for yourself and for a higher purpose, you allow the Divine to manifest miraculous outcomes in your life.

Addiction Is a Spiritual Dilemma

"Man cannot live without joy; therefore, when he is deprived of true spiritual joys it is necessary that he become addicted to carnal pleasures."

~ Thomas Aquinas

Addiction is a challenge not only for those who suffer from it but also for those who love them. The twelve-step program describes addiction—whatever form it takes—as a spiritual dilemma. When we are truly connected to our higher selves and feel fulfilled and sustained by that Divine connection, there is no need to reach outside ourselves to fill an emptiness. That fullness comes from within.

"Every addiction arises from an unconscious refusal to face and move through your own pain. Every addiction starts with pain and ends with pain. Whatever the substance you are addicted to - alcohol, food, legal or illegal drugs, or a person - you are using something or somebody to cover up your pain."

~ Eckhart Tolle

Addiction truly is a painful, lose–lose situation. As Tolle observes, it begins in pain and ends in pain. What makes it even more heartbreaking is that those caught in its grip often cannot easily find their way out. Escaping addiction is anything but simple.

"Facing personal truths and purging yourself of addictions or manipulative habits require strength, courage, humility, faith, and other qualities of a soul with stamina, because you are not just changing yourself; you are changing your universe. Your soul is a compass. Change one coordinate in your spiritual compass and you change your entire life's direction."

~ Caroline Myss

There is deep truth in what these spiritual teachers share. It takes tremendous strength and courage to break free from addictive behavior. You can encourage someone endlessly to let go—whether the addiction is to a person, substance, or habit—but the reality remains: addiction is extremely difficult to release, and the decision to walk away belongs to the one struggling. No one can make that choice for another.

Addicts have a remarkable way of procuring what they crave. Against all odds, when it is time to "pick up," they find it. Deep down, they know it is not the right path, yet it is the path they are on.

If you love someone suffering from addiction, my heart goes out to you. As these teachers remind us, there is often little you can do except pray—pray that the person experiences a spiritual awakening strong enough to help them face the truth, find courage, and begin the journey toward freedom.

Many people have suffered with addiction and eventually found the strength to turn their lives around. They didn't do it alone. They leaned on a higher power—whatever that meant to them—or on a community grounded in that higher power.

If you are suffering from addiction yourself, I encourage you to go inward. Find the courage, strength, and wisdom to take steps toward salvation and relief from the pain you have been carrying—whether that pain is rooted in fear, loss, or trauma that you haven't yet had the courage to face.

Nobody promised life would be easy. Sometimes it is brutally hard. But support exists if you are willing to seek it. Reach out. Ask for help. As the saying goes, *"Ask, and you shall receive."* I believe this to be true. Go within and ask your higher guidance. Ask those who have walked this road before you and have had a spiritual awakening. Do not carry this alone. You can recover.

And remember: we are all born with a Divine Light meant to be shared with the world. Find that light within you. Let it shine brightly. When you do, you not only illuminate your own path but also leave a legacy of courage, hope, and strength for others to follow.

Compassion and Recovery

"Compassion asks us to go where it hurts, to enter into faces of pain, to share in brokenness, fear, confusion, and anguish. Compassion challenges us to cry out with those in misery, to mourn with those who are lonely, to weep with those in tears. Compassion requires us to be weak with the weak, vulnerable with the vulnerable, and powerless with the powerless. Compassion means full immersion into the condition of being human."

~ Henry Nouwen

What does compassion really mean? Henry defines it beautifully. At its core, compassion is the ability to connect with someone in their pain. But how can we truly connect with another's suffering if we've never experienced something similar ourselves?

Consider the loss of a beloved animal—a dog, a cat, or any cherished companion. That kind of loss cuts deeply. You've had this unconditionally loving being by your side for however long—maybe a short time, maybe many years. The length of time doesn't matter. What matters is that they were there: fully loving, innocent, and compassionate. Animals embody pure presence. Unless you've bonded with a pet at that depth and then endured their passing, it is hard to understand the depth of grief others feel when it happens.

This brings me to twelve-step programs and one reason they are so effective. The people in those rooms have been where the newcomers are. They've struggled, they've suffered, and then they found a way forward. They learned how to live—on life's terms. In those meetings, newcomers hear stories of courage, strength, and hope. They discover that recovery is possible because others before them have walked the same path.

That shared experience creates a community of compassion. The people there understand pain at the level Henry describes. They have lived it. They know how devastating it can be. But they also offer something more: the strength and courage that remind others this season of suffering will not last forever. They say, in essence, *"This too shall pass. Healing will come. A new day is ahead and eventually you will get through to the other side of your pain."*

Recovery and relief are not instantaneous. It takes time, patience, and inner work. The key is to honor yourself through the grieving process—to allow space for healing, to treat yourself with grace, give yourself time, and trust that recovery is possible.

Stuck In the Past ~ Rewriting Traumatic Experiences

"Some people are going to love you no matter what you do, and some people will never love you no matter what you do. Go where the love is "

~ Eleanor Brown

The first time I heard this quote, it was modified to: *"Go where the love is, not where you want it to be."* That means we may long for unconditional acceptance and love from our parents or another loved one, but that doesn't mean we're going to receive it. It doesn't mean they are capable of giving it. It doesn't mean they have enough love within themselves to turn around and share it with others.

"There are times in our lives when we have to realize our past is precisely what it is, and we cannot change it, but we can change the story we tell ourselves about it, and by doing that, we can change the future."

~ Eleanor Brown

I love that quote. I believe that if we stay present in the moment and remain conscious of our thoughts—the words we speak, the information we allow into our minds—then we shape both our present and our future. But if we stay focused on the past, letting it consume our present, we remain stuck there.

Of course, sometimes the past can be wonderful, and it's fun to remember those moments. But if your past carries trauma, why not release it? Why not move on and stay present? Why not even rewrite that old story?

I once learned a neuro-linguistic programming process in which the instructor asked us to revisit an uncomfortable life event and reimagine it. So, we did. We replayed the event in our mind's eye and in our memories, but this time we rewrote the story so that we were rescued by a superhero—whoever that was for us. It proved to be a powerful way to transform the memory and change how it feels now. Today, when I think of that unpleasant event, I fondly recall my superhero coming to the rescue. That process shifted the emotional charge from sadness, hurt, and victimhood to triumph and the joy of being saved.

After all, those events live in memory, so why not change the memory to make it lighter? If you rewrite it so that your superhero swoops in to save the day, then when you look back on it, instead of re-experiencing trauma, you might remember a moment of rescue and empowerment. That shift alone can change how the past lives inside you.

So don't let the past interrupt your future—or your now. Stay present in the moment, because when you do, you realize that whatever is happening in your life right now can be shifted. You have the ability to make new plans, to change what needs changing, or to move into acceptance and change the way you think about it until your peace returns.

You could stay stuck and miserable, but why choose that? Instead, show up for God by showing up fully in this moment. Bring your whole self to the present, and you'll create the space for God to show up for you in miraculous ways.

Controversy ~ The Teacher

"Embrace controversy. It gives you a platform. It is a teacher, a clarifier, and your friend, especially if you are trying to make a change." ~ Gloria Feldt

Controversy can be a great teacher. When you take a stand on an issue, you discover who you are and what you stand for. That kind of clarity is essential.

I can also see how controversy, as Feldt says, gives you a platform. When you declare your position, you automatically create a foundation from which to speak and act. It becomes a clarifier as well. By standing firm, you not only learn about yourself but also sharpen your sense of truth and identity. In this way, controversy really can be a friend, especially when you are trying to make a change.

"The ultimate measure of a man is not where he stands in moments of comfort and convenience, but where he stands at times of challenge and controversy."

~ Martin Luther King Jr.

I fully agree. You can tell a great deal about someone not when life is easy but when life is hard.

Take something simple: if a person spills something on their clothing, how they react reveals much about their emotional intelligence. One response might be a shrug—*"Well, that happened."* Another response might be frustration, anger, or embarrassment. The difference shows something about who they are. Now imagine a more serious situation, such as a car accident that destroys your vehicle. How do you respond? Do you resist and rage, or do you accept what has happened and deal with it rationally, with integrity?

Acceptance doesn't mean passivity. It means facing reality as it is: "Yes, the accident happened. Yes, my car is gone. Yes, it will take effort to replace it or have it repaired." Then you ask, *What steps can I take now?* A meltdown doesn't serve you; clear thinking does.

All of us will face controversy, trials, and tribulations—that is part of being human. But in those moments, we can decide: Do I respond by losing control, or do I respond with acceptance and resolve? The choice shapes not only the situation but also who we become in the process.

Resistance to Change ~ Everything Changes

Change is inevitable in life. You can either resist it and potentially get run over by it, or you can choose to cooperate with it, adapt to it, and learn how to benefit from it. When you embrace change you will begin to see it as an opportunity for growth.

~ Jack Canfield

I want to talk about change. Even when something is shifting for the better, we often feel an inner resistance. It's a curious thing—knowing that circumstances are improving can be exciting, yet at the same time anxiety, stress, or even a fight-or-flight response may arise. Why, if we know the change benefits us? Simply because it's change. Stepping out of our comfort zone can feel unsettling, even traumatic for some, regardless of whether the outcome is positive.

Some changes may look negative on the surface, but in time you may realize they are creating space for something new to emerge. Personally, I love that. Right now, things in my own life are changing. I know it's for the better, and I accept that, but I still found resistance rising within me. I had to come to a place of complete acceptance—of *what is* now, of what is unfolding, and of what will be—to be at peace with it, excited about it, and grateful that it's happening.

It fascinates me that even when I know change is for the better, I still feel antsy. Life is like that—interesting, unpredictable, and sometimes difficult to accept. Of course not everyone experiences change this way. Some people thrive on it. I know people who leap into change eagerly, thrilled for the next adventure. Maybe that describes you— and if so, wonderful. For many of us, though, change can be overwhelming and disconcerting, even when we understand it's ultimately for our good.

Understanding Loss ~ Time Heals All Wounds

"Even a happy life cannot be without a measure of darkness, and the word happy would lose its meaning if it were not balanced by sadness."

~ Carl Jung

In order to know happiness, we must also know sadness. If we had never faced difficulties, would we truly understand— or relate to—others going through hard times? Would we have compassion for them? Would we fully appreciate the good moments?

Jonathan Safran Foer wrote in *Everything Is Illuminated*, "You cannot protect yourself from sadness without also protecting yourself from happiness." Experiencing loss is part of the human condition. At some point, each of us will face it, and with loss often comes sadness and grief. That is okay. Loss and change are inevitable. For many, change can be deeply challenging—especially for those who have lived through trauma and work hard to keep everything calm, controlled, and drama-free. Their desire to maintain emotional stability is understandable, particularly when reminders of past pain evoke intense physical or emotional reactions.

If you are having a moment of sadness, allow yourself to fully feel it. Sadness will come, and joy will return too. Remember: you wouldn't feel such deep grief if you hadn't also known deep joy. Bringing happy memories into your mind can help soften the sorrow. It is right to feel sadness; it is also important not to dwell there.

A good friend of mine lost his wife after forty-six years of marriage. I imagine the void he feels when he comes home to a quiet, empty house. For anyone experiencing such loss, my heart goes out to you. Know that these feelings will pass— sometimes slowly, sometimes quickly—but they will shift. In time, the memories that once brought tears will more often bring smiles. You will experience joy again. You will find happiness again.

When my father passed away, it took nearly two years before I could speak of him without breaking down in tears. Time does heal wounds. Time does help us with the losses. You will get through your sadness. You will move on to better times.

For now, give yourself grace. Take the time you need to heal and adjust to life as it is now. Be compassionate with yourself. Allow yourself time to grieve, to rest, to heal, and to rediscover your center.

And as you do, let the joy-filled memories surface. Remember the laughter, the smiles, the moments of love. Reminisce about your happy times often. Those memories are treasures—proof of the love that shaped you and reminders that happiness will find you again.

Facing Your Problems Head On ~ Critical Thinking Skills

"Most people spend more time and energy going around problems than in trying to solve them."

~ Henry Ford

Avoiding a problem doesn't make it go away, and trying to go around it doesn't make it go away either. The best approach is to face the problem directly and determine how to change things so that it no longer remains a problem.

"Learn to use your brainpower; critical thinking is the key to creative problem-solving in business."

~ Richard Branson

I couldn't agree more. Critical thinking is essential. It means analyzing situations and viewing them from different perspectives. That's the foundation of Socratic questioning— exploring issues from multiple angles. If you're struggling with a decision, one way to shift perspective is to ask, *If this were my best friend, what would I recommend they do?* More often than not, the answer will differ from your own initial thought because you've stepped outside of yourself and changed your viewpoint.

"We cannot solve our problems with the same thinking we used when we created them."

~ Albert Einstein

Einstein's point is profound: to change outcomes, we must change our thinking. How do we do that? We start by looking at the problem from another perspective. Lay out the pros and cons: What's working in this situation? What isn't?

Even more important, we can go inward. By shifting from the head to the heart, we open ourselves to inner guidance— insights we might miss if we rely solely on analytical thought. When we bring a situation into our heart center, sit with it, and ask for divine direction, we can often discern the next best step. The key is to listen for that answer.

My hope is that this encourages you to adjust your perspective, explore new viewpoints, and, most importantly, tune in. What is your intuition saying? What is your divine guidance offering? What is the next best step to move forward and resolve the problem?

STAGE 2

Searching
for Truth

Searching for Answers

And the search begins. You seek out books on making a difference, leaving a legacy, being of service, and living a life of passion—self-help books like *The Law of Attraction, The Power of Now, The Anatomy of Spirit, The Power of Intention, The Purpose Driven Life, Life on the Other Side, The Seven Laws of Spiritual Success, Opening to Channel,* and more. You become an avid reader, a dedicated student, searching for meaning and answers.

You attend workshops and retreats. You purchase crystals, incense, essential oils, and candles. You learn about meditation, channeling, and energy. You practice yoga, tai chi, qigong, and quieting the mind. You check in with psychics and channels, attend ceremonies, sweat lodges, and spiritual gatherings.

You learn a lot. And yet—you still don't find what you are looking for.

What's Missing? ~ A Spiritual Connection

It's all spirit and it's all connected. Our choice is to live out of harmony with spiritual ways or in harmony with spiritual ways. Everything is spiritual.

~ William Commanda

I did a little research to see what happens when someone becomes disconnected from their spirituality or inner guidance. What I found was disconcerting, and I want to share it with you.

Common symptoms of spiritual disconnection include a lack of purpose or meaning, feelings of isolation or loneliness, loss of hope or optimism, heightened stress or anxiety, overwhelm, emotional imbalance, lack of self-awareness and self-reflection, loss of a moral compass, and confusion or ethical dilemmas.

Looking at that list, I realized many people may be quietly suffering. If any of these symptoms resonate with you—if you feel cut off from your inner guidance, your higher self, your guardian angels, or the wisdom that flows from divine connection and inspiration—I encourage you to consider working with a spiritual coach who can help you rebuild that connection.

This is inner work. It is the process of reconnecting with the resources already within you. When you tune in to your inner guidance, you may rediscover direction and begin forming deep, meaningful connections with others. Those connections foster hope and optimism and provide strength for difficult times. Over time, they build a strong spiritual foundation— beliefs and practices that bring peace and tranquility.

If you know someone struggling with symptoms of disconnection, reach out. Help them find a spiritual coach or someone with the insight and ability to guide them back to their inner strength and to the Source that resides in all of us.

We are each born with divine gifts meant to be shared with the world. That divinity is within us, even if we are not always fully connected to it. But if you cannot connect at all—if you feel stuck, lonely, or adrift without a moral compass—please don't isolate yourself. Have the courage to reach out for help. Find someone who can help you strengthen your intuitive, spiritual connection. It is within you; you may simply need to uncover it again.

Spiritual Questioning

"The meaning of life is to find your gift. The purpose of life is to give it away."

~ Pablo Picasso

And then the questions begin: What is life all about? How do I find meaning? These questions can arise at any age—youth or old age makes no difference. I've known people to awaken in their sixties, and I've met eighteen-year-olds who are already awake. I've even met children who were wide awake. In fact, I believe children are born awake, and in our society, we are conditioned to shut them down—to put them to sleep, so to speak.

The questions come, and the answers often seem obscure. This is when the "teacher" appears. And the teacher comes with even more questions—questions that can sometimes feel perplexing, such as: "What are you passionate about? Where do you see yourself five years from now? What would you like your obituary to say? What is truly important to you? Do you want your life to matter? Do you want to make a difference?"

The Universe Conspires on Our Behalf ~ For Us, Not Against Us

"Life is simple. Everything happens for you, not to you. Everything happens at exactly the right moment, neither too soon nor too late. You don't have to like it... it's just easier if you do."

~ Byron Katie

There are moments when it feels as if life is against us—or even that people are conspiring against us. Yet, as Byron Katie suggests, these experiences are not punishments; they are invitations meant to encourage introspection. Each challenge urges us to delve deeper within ourselves to uncover what aspects of our being might be attracting such situations so that we can grow from them. A happy, successful life is all about personal growth; it is shaped by how we respond to our difficulties, how we evolve, and how we navigate the world around us.

We may not always like what unfolds, and it may never feel comfortable in the moment. But when we embrace the idea that life is happening for us rather than to us, everything shifts. Each event presents an opportunity for us to scrutinize our inner dynamics, to pinpoint what might be drawing these circumstances into our lives, and from there, we can choose to grow as we embark on a journey of transformation.

This process enables us to modify our behavior, fostering growth and change within ourselves. We can reshape the patterns that dictate what we attract into our lives. It's about evolving, digging deeper, and perhaps becoming more committed to being our best selves—to making choices that align with integrity and positive action. In doing so, we not only grow—we also show up for God, allowing Him to guide and transform us in miraculous ways.

Ah-Hah ~ The Answers Are Within

"I try not to listen to the shoulds or coulds and try to get beyond expectations, peer pressure, or trying to please— and just listen. I believe all the answers are ultimately within us."

~ Kim Cattrall

And then one day, when you least expect it—when you've "given up" on having the answers, when the inquiring, egoic mind steps aside—something happens. Like someone flipping a switch, in the flick of a moment, you get it. You understand. Perhaps it comes from one of the dozens of books you've read, something you've heard from a channel, or a quiet moment of meditation.

It hits you: the answers are within you. You are the one with the answers—not your ego self, not your egoic mind. Not the voice in your head that says, "You should do…" or "You'll never do that," or "That will never happen," or "You're crazy." Not that voice. No. Amid the din of all the voices in your head, you begin to hear the one that speaks with truth, grace, and love—the voice of your higher self, your soul, your spiritual guide, your guardian angel, your master teacher, your divine inner guidance.

"As you awaken, you will come to understand that the journey to love is about becoming the one, not finding the one."

~ Craig Crippen

We are all becoming "the one" at this time of transformation of the world.

'Nothing is about finding anything outside of ourselves; everything is about becoming that which we seek. Don't look for love; become love. Don't look for happiness; be happy. Don't look for kindness; be kind. Don't look for change; become the change. Life is an inside job; our soul has the answers.'

~ Laura Abilene

Our souls have the answers. This is the basic premise of coaching: coaches ask questions because our clients already have the answers within. You have the answers. Your soul has the answers.

Life is an inside job. Our soul's love energy leads the way. Pay attention to the messages coming from your soul. Your instincts will guide you—listen to your intuition. What is it telling you? Have faith. Tune in to your soul for wisdom and guidance.

I believe we all possess a divine spark of intuition, inner guidance, and wisdom. This divine knowledge is available to everyone. All we need to do is tune in and ask: What am I meant to do? What am I called to do? What message am I meant to share with others? What are my innate gifts—those meant to be manifested and shared with the world?

Perhaps it is time, in the evolution of our species, for all of us to tap into our souls and begin giving back—to start making a difference in the world.

I believe our time has come. It's time to step up—to step into who we are meant to be. Not to be influenced by what someone else tells us we should do, but to trust our own inner guidance. Have faith that the message your soul is giving you, and the steps you are intuitively guided to take, are exactly what you are meant to do—now.

Be brave. Be bold. Step into it wholeheartedly. Follow your inner guidance.

We are all born to manifest the divine wisdom, guidance, and gifts we have been given. Now is the time to walk the path of your divine purpose and share it with the world.

Show up for God, and God will show up for you in miraculous ways. Be ready to share your gifts—they are amazing, mind-blowing, and life-changing. You will love your life when you fully show up for God in this way.

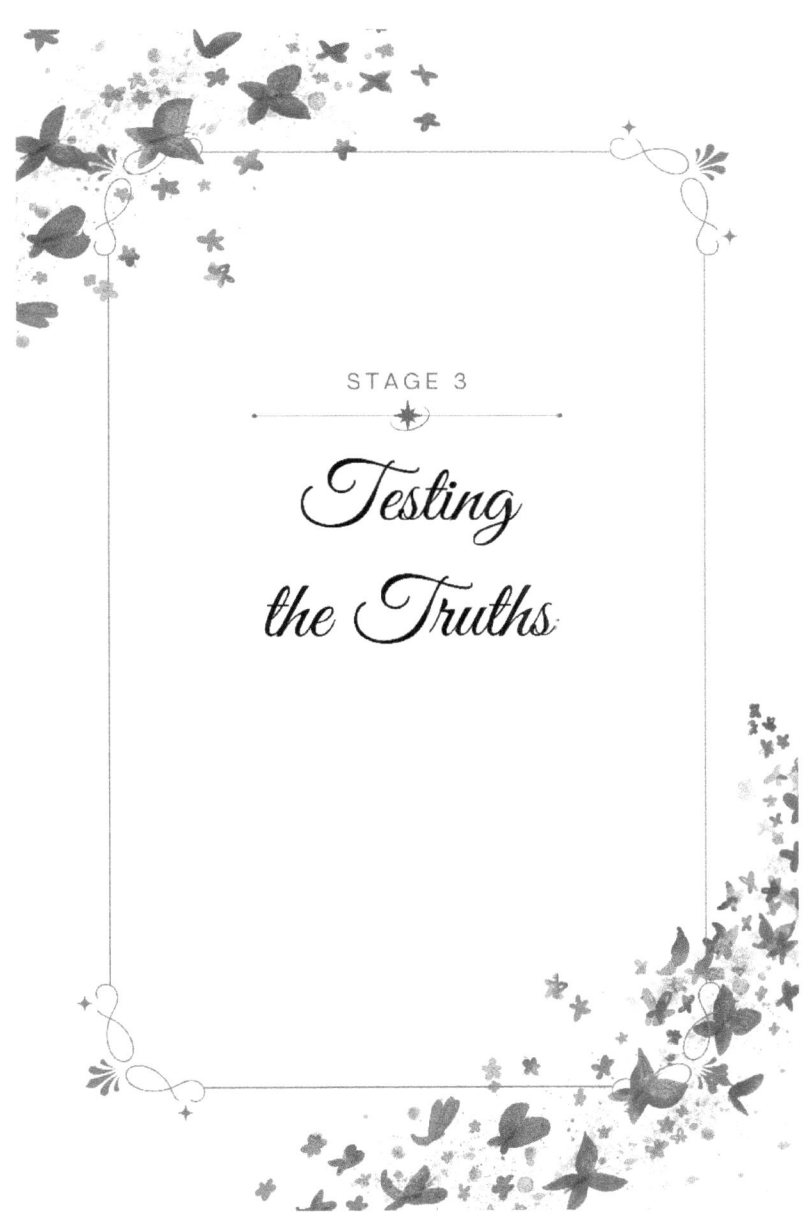

STAGE 3

Testing the Truths

Out of the Dark and Into the Light ~
The Meaning of Life

Once the missing pieces are found—such as the understanding that "our thoughts create our reality"—the next step is to test that. This involves monitoring one's thoughts to see if they can manifest something, effectively testing whether metaphysics are true and whether thoughts indeed create reality.

During your spiritual quest, you learned about things called "universal truths" or "universal laws." Some of these ideas were hard to swallow—like, "Your thoughts create your reality." What? Really? Who wants to believe that?

Think about it: most of us began this spiritual journey because we weren't thrilled with the reality we were living in. We were frustrated, stuck, or just plain unhappy. And now we're supposed to accept that we created all of that—with our own thoughts? Ouch.

It's a tough pill to swallow. It's one thing to read about it in a book or hear it in a lecture; it's another to actually look at your own life and realize that your thoughts, beliefs, and energy played a role in shaping the world you've been struggling in. Suddenly, spirituality isn't just about changing your reality—it's about taking full responsibility for it. And that can be scary, humbling, and, oddly enough, empowering all at once.

The Influence of Thought

"People need to realize that their thoughts are more primary than their genes, because the environment, which is influenced by our thoughts, controls the genes."

~ Bruce H. Lipton

This quote from Bruce Lipton is both powerful and eye-opening. If you haven't come across his work before, I encourage you to look him up on YouTube—his talks are truly remarkable. What he's saying here is simple but profound: our thoughts don't just shape how we feel in the moment; they can actually influence our biology. Our thoughts influence our environment, and our environment guides our genetic expression.

Think about that. Most of us were taught that our genes are set in stone—that they control our lives, our health, and even our future. Lipton, however, shows us that our genes are not fixed. Instead, they respond to the environment we live in. And what shapes that environment more than anything else? Our thoughts.

When we think loving, positive thoughts, we create a healthier environment inside and around us. When we think negative or fearful thoughts, we create a very different environment—one that can weaken us over time. In this way, our thoughts act like the switch that turns genes on or off.

While still not widely known, this knowledge is empowering. It reminds us that we are not victims of our DNA; we are co-creators of our reality. The more we stay conscious and intentional with our thoughts, the more aligned we become with joy, health, and purpose. Align your thoughts with your passions and purpose, and you set the stage for a more fulfilling life.

When your actions flow from your authentic self, joy becomes a natural companion. And when you let your inner light shine, you not only transform your own life—you illuminate the path for others.

The Power of Positive Thinking

"I believe you are robbing the world of who you are when you have a gift to share with others but let fear hold you back from expressing it.¹"

~ Lewis Holmes

"You weren't an accident; you weren't mass-produced. You aren't an assembly-line product; you were deliberately planned, so specifically gifted and lovingly positioned on the Earth by the master Craftsman."

~ Max Lucado

What you do with your giftedness is ultimately up to you. Yet if fear takes hold—if you find yourself thinking, *What if I take this step? What will happen?*—I encourage you to play the movie forward. Imagine the possibilities all the way to the end. What is the best that could happen? What is the worst?

Notice how different those paths feel. When you focus on the best outcomes, the emotions that rise within you are inspiring, powerful, and energizing. But when you dwell on the worst possibilities, those feelings bring heavy emotions.

This is the essence of positive thinking: our thoughts create our reality. If you choose thoughts that are uplifting, you will feel good, motivated, and empowered. If you choose negative thoughts, you will feel discouraged and stuck. By directing your mind toward positive possibilities, you prepare yourself to take bold steps forward. When the time comes to act, your first thoughts will be ones of confidence, success, and momentum—thoughts that keep you inspired, committed, and moving in the direction that lifts you up.

Your Thoughts Create Your Reality

"Change your thinking, change your life. Your thoughts create your reality. Practice positive thinking, act the way you want to be, and soon you will be the way you act."

~ Les Brown

Your thoughts create your reality. If you sit with that idea for a moment, you'll recognize the undeniable truth in it. Our thoughts don't just pass through our minds—they shape our lives. As the old saying goes, "As a man thinketh, so is he." In other words, not only do our thoughts create our reality, but our consciously aware thoughts can empower and uplift us.

On the flip side, if we're not mindful, our thoughts can also harm us—and sometimes others as well. I recall an exercise my friend Helice "Sparky" Bridges often leads. She asks people to send loving energy to someone, then measures the impact through muscle testing. Loving energy produces strong, resilient responses. Next, she has them send negative energy—and the muscle test shows weakness. It's a simple yet profound demonstration of how our energy field is influenced by the thoughts and emotions we project.

Recognizing the immense power of our thoughts is crucial. Loving, compassionate thoughts attract more love and vibrant energy into your life. Negative thoughts, however, create a different energetic imprint—one that diminishes well-being. And really, who wouldn't want to cultivate more love, more vitality, more life-giving energy?

This is why it's so important to acknowledge that your thoughts do create your reality. By maintaining a positive mindset and focusing on what you truly want to create and experience, you align yourself with joy, fulfillment, and inner peace. And in doing so, you begin paving the way toward a life you genuinely love.

Testing Manifestation and Intuition

So we test the idea that our thoughts create our reality. We focus our thoughts. We begin with little things—a parking space close to the door, a string of green lights while we're driving. We think of someone we haven't talked to in a while and expect a call; then we watch the clock to see how long it takes before the phone rings.

Little by little, we see the results of our efforts—and we're amazed. It dawns on us that our thoughts might indeed influence the events of our lives. We begin to see that not only did we create much of our reality, we made choices before we incarnated into the physical body we now inhabit. We chose our parents, our environment, our life experiences, our friends, our families, our life situation. We chose it all.

Almost simultaneously, we wonder, *What was I thinking when I chose this life?* Then our intuition kicks in, and we remember: we made those choices before we incarnated, when we were in our true state as spiritual beings. At the time, we clearly had no idea how difficult those choices would feel once we arrived in a body and forgot who we really were.

Manifestation

Our subconscious minds have no sense of humor, play no jokes and cannot tell the difference between reality and an imagined thought or image. What we continually think about eventually will manifest in our lives.

~ Robert Collier

When we focus our attention and perspective—when we choose to see life through the lens of abundance, trusting that the universe is perfect and always conspiring on our behalf to provide exactly what we need at the perfect moment—miracles begin to unfold. The more we hold that intention and keep that focus, the more we invite miracles that bless us in truly miraculous ways.

Ask yourself: *What is the next best thing that could happen for me? What would light me up? What would make my day if it came to pass?* Focus your intention on that vision and begin to see it as your reality. Every day, remind yourself of this beautiful, wonderful experience already making its way toward you. Act as though you already have it. Say to yourself: *Yes, I have it now. It's here. It's real. I can feel it. I can taste it.* In your mind's eye, imagine how wonderful your life is now.

This practice will serve you in the highest way possible. It accelerates the unfolding of your desires far more effectively than worry ever could. Worry only delays you; it does not take you where you want to go. But imagining, visualizing, and embodying your desires as though they already exist generates the energy that draws them into your life. When you align your inner vision with your faith, you attract exactly what you are seeking—right here, right now.

Master Your Thoughts Through Self-Discipline

"Self-discipline begins with the mastery of your thoughts. If you don't control what you think, you can't control what you do. Simply, self-discipline enables you to think first and act afterward."

~ Napoleon Hill

"Thinking is a habit, and like any other habit, it can be changed; it just takes effort and repetition."

~ John Eliot

"Change your thoughts through repetition and the creation of "habits," which is the primary way we acquire subconscious programs after age 7. This can't just be sticky notes on the mirror. This must be felt and experienced. "

~ Bruce Lipton

These three quotes all emphasize the significance of introspection and awareness of our thoughts. They encourage us to become conscious of our thinking patterns and to recognize how those patterns influence our actions.

Self-discipline begins with the regulation of thought. If we want to govern our actions, we must first learn to manage our thinking—our minds. True self-discipline is the practice of pausing, of choosing to think before taking action. Ultimately, your response to any situation is your responsibility—your *response-ability*.

The encouraging news is that thinking itself is a habit—and habits can change. Our thought patterns are malleable. Just like any other habit, thinking can be altered through persistence and repetition. I urge you to become a conscious observer of your thoughts and to distinguish between empowering and disempowering ones. Cancel the disempowering thoughts and reinforce the empowering ones.

Repetition is the key to shaping the subconscious. Internalize thoughts that uplift and empower you through consistent repetition. Habits form through consistent practice, so practice mindfulness and train your mind to think good thoughts.

As you begin observing your thoughts, you will often notice ego-based ones that hinder your progress and hold you back—thoughts that are self-critical, limiting, or rooted in comparison. To counteract these, immerse yourself in uplifting content that fosters positive reprogramming. Through the repetition of empowering ideas, old subconscious patterns that block your success can be replaced.

Becoming the observer of your thoughts empowers you to discern between ego-driven and inspiration-driven thinking. Ego-based thoughts tend to limit you, while inspired thoughts propel you forward. Acting on inspired thoughts aligns you with your highest good and opens the door to transformative experiences.

To transcend the ego-mind is to enter stillness. This is the ultimate awakening. When we become the silent witness of our own mind-generated thoughts, we can evaluate and decide whether they are worth expressing—or not. Are they uplifting, empowering, expansive, higher-mind thoughts? Or are they complaining, comparative, or regret-filled ego thoughts—"should have, would have, could have"? Once you pay attention, it becomes easier to discern whether your thoughts come from the ego-mind or the higher mind. From that awareness, you gain the freedom to choose which thoughts to express and which to release. Strive to be as conscious and awakened as you possibly can, so that you own the power and freedom to choose.

Remember, when your thoughts and actions align, you embody integrity and remain true to your word. Your journey of conscious action is not only transformative for yourself but also inspirational to others. By honoring your sacred thoughts and acting on them, you show up for God—and, in turn, invite miraculous outcomes into your life.

Destiny or Subconscious Programming?

"Luck becomes a convenient excuse when things don't go your way, and luck is a rationale for staying comfortable while you wait for luck to determine your fate."

~ Tim Grover

Here's the thing about luck: life is what you make of it. I wouldn't say it was luck that helped Edison figure out how to make a lightbulb work. He tried 999 times or so before he actually succeeded. Was that luck? I don't think so.

I believe we have to work for what we want. And if we are "in our lane"—doing what comes naturally to us—then the work feels effortless. However, if we find ourselves struggling, that may be an indication of subconscious programming working against us. So, I don't really believe in luck, *per se.* When someone appears very successful, it's because they've done the work. Perhaps it looked effortless because they were aligned with their destiny or divine providence, which guided them into what they were called to do.

If you feel inner resistance to what you know you are meant to do—if you can sense it in your bones and your intuition tells you to take the step, yet fear or resistance holds you back—that is a good indication that your subconscious programming isn't aligned with your true path. That's when I recommend working with a coach who can help you break through the barriers that keep you from stepping fully into what you are meant to give back to the world.

What gifts do you have to offer the world? Carl Jung said, "Until you make the unconscious conscious, it will direct your life and you will call it fate." Is it truly fate, or is it your unconscious mind driving your decisions and choices that could ultimately be holding you back from stepping into and becoming the extraordinary human being that you're meant to be? If subconscious programming is influencing your life, working with a coach can help you achieve those much-needed breakthroughs. My favorite part of my coaching classes is witnessing those moments of transformation—when the students experience their own breakthroughs while learning how to facilitate them for others.

Is your subconscious mind holding you back from stepping into your greatness—from sharing your unique gifts with the world? If the urge to create is within you, then that creation is meant to be expressed. Don't suppress the feelings. Instead, embrace and honor the gifts God has entrusted to you. Ask yourself: What steps can I take to bring this into being—sooner rather than later?

Reprogramming Your Subconscious

"Whatever we plant in our subconscious mind and nourish with repetition and emotion will one day become a reality."

~ Earl Nightingale

I believe that most people sabotage themselves or have an inner resistance to moving forward with what is in their creative, conscious mind—what they truly want to do. They resist taking action because it conflicts with what is in their subconscious mind.

Emotions are energy in motion. Our feelings and emotions can deceive and sabotage us because of our subconscious programming. Our subconscious mind is programmed when we are very young, and unless we take steps to reprogram it through repetition, we continue to struggle with fulfilling what we are truly called to do.

"Your conscious desires and your subconscious intention must be in alignment. If your conscious mind wants one thing and the subconscious mind wants something else, it's impossible to create what you truly want."

~ Robert Anthony

Until your subconscious mind is on board with your *soul mission*, your emotions may influence your thoughts, and you may create experiences that don't serve your highest good. When you reprogram your subconscious mind with what your creative, conscious self truly wants to accomplish, you will naturally create that experience. You will also naturally take the steps that move you forward in your life. It's not complicated—it's actually very simple. When your subconscious and creative consciousness are in alignment, you can experience the breakthrough to success you both deserve and are meant to achieve.

You can live a life you absolutely love—and help others live a life they love as well. It all comes down to reprogramming the subconscious mind so it aligns with where the creative, conscious mind wants to go. Then you can easily and naturally step into who you are at your core, express that, and gift it back to the world. That is why we are all here: to share our gifts with the world.

So—what are your gifts? What is stopping you? Most likely, it's old programming in your subconscious mind that isn't in alignment with where you are meant to go.

I always say that what is inside of you is meant to be gifted back to the world. That's one reason for writing this book. I am practicing what I preach: *Show Up for God and God Will Show Up for You in Miraculous Ways.* As soon as we begin taking divine steps toward manifesting what we are meant to gift back, God lays the way straight before us—opening doors and magnetically attracting the right people and the right experiences to help us succeed.

Filter On Glimmers

"Have you heard about glimmers? They are the opposite of triggers. A glimmer is a tiny micro moment of happiness, a sign of hope. Once you begin to look for them, they will start to appear everywhere." ~ Deb Dana

This is so true. Our minds naturally filter for certain things—that's simply how they work. For example, when you're about to buy a car, suddenly it seems as though everyone on the road is driving that same car. Or, if you decide to notice butterflies, they begin to appear all around you—on signs, in books, and in nature. Our attention gravitates toward what we focus on.

The same is true of glimmers. When you consciously look for them, you begin to notice them everywhere—those tiny, beautiful moments that light you up: a gentle breeze, leaves fluttering in the wind, a fresh flower in bloom, the sparkle of sunlight on water, a smile from a stranger.

What lights you up? What makes you feel good at the end of the day? What makes you smile? What makes your heart sing? Start paying attention to the glimmers, and your mind will begin to filter for them.

Before long, your life will be filled with glimmers—moments of happiness—and soon you'll find yourself living a joy-filled life. It won't just be tiny microcosms of happiness; it will be a life infused with joy and light all the time.

Happiness By Design

Success is not the key to happiness. Happiness is the key to success. If you love what you are doing, you will be successful."

~ Albert Schweitzer

I wholeheartedly agree with Albert Schweitzer's sentiment. It mirrors my own experience: I have a deep passion for teaching the art and skill of coaching. Witnessing those "aha" moments in others brings me profound happiness, and I feel tremendously blessed to earn a living doing what I truly love.

Dr. Bruce Lipton offers a powerful reminder that happiness is not something we stumble upon—it can be consciously created. He suggests a deceptively simple practice: if you want to experience happiness, say aloud, *I'm happy*, every day for thirty days. Outwardly, your circumstances may not yet reflect this reality, but the words are not meant for the outside world—they are meant for your subconscious mind. Through the repetition of this declaration, your subconscious begins to accept it, and in time, happiness becomes your lived experience.

The process is beautifully simple. Keep affirming *I'm happy* until your subconscious fully embraces it. Eventually, your thoughts, feelings, and actions align with this truth. Happiness, then, is not just a fleeting state but the foundation upon which success is built.

I encourage you: begin today. Plant the seed of happiness in your subconscious, nourish it with repetition and emotion, and watch as it grows into a reality that not only transforms your own life but also inspires others around you.

Practicing
the Principles

Exploration and Discovery

After successfully testing and gaining confidence in this knowledge—saying to yourself, "I've tested it. Check it out. Look what I created. I manifested. I made something happen."—the next natural step is to begin to practice principles such as honesty, integrity, truth, congruency, being true to your word, following through, commitment, and consistency.

With the realization that we create our reality through our thoughts—now tested and proven—you may be curious to explore other esoteric concepts: mass consciousness, multiverses, simultaneous time nodes, the physical plane, the etheric plane, the astral plane, the causal plane, the mental plane, the spiritual realm, the soul connection, the oversoul, and the vortex. These concepts are offered here as food for thought, though we will not explore them in depth in this book.

Instead, our focus will be on core spiritual principles: honesty, integrity, trust, congruency, forgiveness, acceptance, commitment, consistency, and the practice of accepting responsibility.

Honesty & Integrity

"Honesty and integrity are absolutely essential for success in all areas of life. The really good news is that anyone can develop both honesty and integrity."

- Zig Ziglar

In *Alcoholics Anonymous: The Big Book*, Chapter five notes that some people are incapable of being honest with themselves—and I believe that is true. I've known individuals who struggle deeply with honesty, not only with others but also with themselves. In most cases, some form of addiction is present. In fact, I have never personally known anyone who battled addiction without also grappling with issues of honesty.

That said, I agree with Zig Ziglar that honesty and integrity can be developed by anyone willing to make the choice. To me, being true to your word and congruent with your actions is vital when it comes to being honest and demonstrating integrity.

When you say you are going to do something, do it. This alignment between word and deed is essential. Equally important is to mean what you say and say what you mean— without being mean. Confronting someone should always be done with compassion and love. When you speak the truth without anger or attack, you might be surprised by their response. When you take ownership of your part in a situation and approach the conversation with kindness, you create the possibility for mutual understanding and resolution. Often, the other person may not have even realized their behavior was hurtful or bothersome.

Ultimately, honesty is about congruence—your words must align with your actions. And when you encounter people whose words and actions consistently do not match, it may be time to reevaluate that relationship. Choose to surround yourself with people of integrity—those who are honest, true to their word, and consistent in their actions.

Learning To Trust

"Building trust is a process. Trust results from consistent and predictable interaction over time."

~ Barbara M. White

"The best way to find out if you can trust somebody is to trust them."

~ Ernest Hemingway

Establishing trust requires careful observation of people's actions. It is essential that their words and commitments align with their behavior in order to foster genuine trust.

Hemingway's advice is compelling, yet it raises an important question: How can we trust someone without first having evidence of their trustworthiness? It's prudent to begin gradually—start with smaller tasks or commitments and observe how consistently the person follows through. Watch for signs of honesty, integrity, and reliability. As Barbara White reminds us, trust develops through consistent and predictable actions over time.

By first entrusting someone with modest responsibilities, you create opportunities to assess whether they honor their promises. Over time, as they demonstrate reliability, you can extend greater trust for larger responsibilities. Discernment plays a crucial role here—extend trust gradually for bigger tasks based on the track record they establish through their actions.

This same process applies to developing trust in your intuition. Just as you take small steps to build your confidence in others, you can take manageable actions based on your intuitive nudges. When those actions lead to positive outcomes, your trust in your inner guidance grows stronger.

In both relationships and personal growth, trust is built gradually. It requires patience, discernment, and consistent action. By approaching it this way, you honor not only yourself but also your higher purpose. Trust, once earned and strengthened, becomes one of your most valuable assets.

Trusting Your Inner Guidance

"Anyone who doesn't take truth seriously in small matters cannot be trusted in large ones either."

~ Albert Einstein

Think about that quote. It matters. We need to recognize when someone is telling the truth, and we also need to know our own truth. Discernment is essential—and it develops through life experience. Over time, we learn to sense when someone is being honest and when they are not.

"Be courageous and face this moment in time consciously and with all the discernment and clarity within your power."

~ James O'Dea

James O'Dea said it well. But how do we actually cultivate that discernment and clarity? That is the key question—and one worth answering. It is important for us to understand and learn so we can grow in wisdom and trust.

One way is by developing our intuition. Intuition gives us an internal compass that allows us to test and confirm what feels right and true.

There are four primary modalities of intuition:

- **Clairvoyance**—perceiving images or visions, like a mental movie.

- **Claircognizance**—simply knowing something without logical explanation.
- **Clairaudience**—hearing inner guidance, often as words or phrases.
- **Clairsentience**—experiencing a gut feeling or physical sensation about a situation.

By tuning in, you can ask: *Is this right for me? Is this true for me? Will this be a wise move? Can I trust this person to follow through?*

Throughout my life, I've had people make promises they didn't keep. Over time, I learned to recognize empty promises and to rely on intuition to discern the difference.

That's why I encourage you to check in with your inner guidance when making decisions. Ask yourself: *Is this true for me? Is this my next best step? What other ways could I approach this? How else might I see this situation?* By questioning, you expand your perspective and strengthen your discernment.

I don't recommend seeking guidance from just anyone. Not all people are "safe" people. Some may discourage you out of jealousy, fear, or their own limitations. What you are called to create and give back to the world might trigger resistance in others.

What matters most when you are about to take a leap of faith is trusting your inner guidance that you are moving in the right direction. That trust grows over time. You can ask for confirmation—and you will receive it.

If doors easily fly wide open, that's a sign you're on the right path—keep moving forward. On the other hand, if you keep hitting a wall, if obstacles continually block your way—closed doors, endless delays, even something as small as a car that won't start—it may be guidance that this plan is not in your best interest.

Pay attention to the signs. Ask for confirmation. Trust your intuition. With practice and experience, you will strengthen that trust, and it will become one of your greatest allies.

Ask For a Sign

"As you evolve and develop your psychic abilities, you will enter into perceptions of life, truth, beauty and you will gain power to live your life in an intelligent, perceptive and strong way."

~ Frederick Lenz

As we pursue our divine purpose, we are often given signs confirming that we're on the right path. If you're uncertain about your next step, you can always ask for guidance: *"Is this my next best move? If it is, please give me a sign."*

That sign can be whatever feels meaningful to you. Perhaps it's a butterfly on a book cover, a penny that appears out of nowhere, or an unexpected conversation. However it comes, confirmation will arrive. As we evolve, we can increasingly rely on intuition—the intelligent awareness Frederick Lenz describes.

Intuition often nudges us to move in a certain direction, even when the reason isn't immediately clear. Later, we usually discover why. Sometimes we may get a feeling—or a sense of urgency—that we need to do something. If you're unsure about your intuitive guidance, ask for confirmation. Many spiritual seekers I know do this regularly. They'll ask questions such as: *"Is this the right move for me? Should I take this call? Should I attend this meeting?"*

Asking for confirmation can be as simple as saying: *"Give me a sign that this is the right choice. Let me know I'm on the right path."* You can even be specific: *"I want to see a butterfly in flight."* Soon after, you might see one in nature, on a book cover, or even hear someone mention butterflies out of the blue. Signs may appear in many forms.

Tune in to your intuition. Ask for confirmation. Watch for signs.

Remember, you get to choose what your confirmation will be. One of my teachers chose an airplane flying overhead as her signal from higher guidance. A student once asked for something "electrical" as his sign—only to have the power in his house go out. It was a huge confirmation, but also highly inconvenient! Choose your signs wisely.

Years ago, I posted the following quote on Facebook:

God, grant me serenity as I open to receive abundantly. Grace me with the courage and inner strength to ask for more and to receive more. Bless me with Your Divine Wisdom to know I am worthy and loved. For who am I to judge my value, and who am I to judge the value I am destined to bring to the world?

That message reappeared at exactly the right moment. I was stepping into something far outside my comfort zone—something I knew I was called to do—yet I felt inner resistance. Reading those words was confirmation. I had been asking for courage, for inner strength, for guidance to show up in a bigger way. And here was my prayer reminding me I was meant for more—reminding me not to judge.

Think about this for yourself. Are you being nudged to show up in a bigger way? Is God—or the Universe, or whatever name you give your Higher Power—inviting you to give back more? Perhaps you've been holding back because you haven't yet allowed yourself to receive more. Are you ready to open to what the Universe has in store for you? Are you ready to ask for more so you can show up fully in the way your soul is calling you to?

Take a moment to check in with your higher self. Close your eyes. Breathe deeply. Focus on your inner wisdom and ask: *"Am I open and willing to receive more so I can show up in a bigger way for those who need me?"*

As your intuition evolves, you will notice that life begins to feel like a symphony of synchronicities. You think of someone—and suddenly they call. You arrive somewhere by "chance," only to meet the very person who can help you take your next step. These are not accidents. They are divine appointments. The Universe conspires on our behalf to manifest the people, places, and things we need so that we can easily create our divine purpose and deliver it to the world. The doors open for us at just the right time, allowing us to walk in and either give to the world or receive what we most need.

Watch For the Signs

It's fascinating how the Universe works and how intricately everything is connected. When we become aware of these connections, we begin to notice synchronicities as they occur—and those synchronicities can serve as powerful guidance. The Universe offers signs to all of us. Our task is to watch for them, become aware of them, and respond accordingly. These signs are both teachers and guides along the way.

Consider this: a traffic jam—a sign to stop or slow down—may be the very thing that keeps you from arriving too early, or it may position you to arrive at just the right time. Perhaps it allows you to meet the right person, have the right conversation, or take the next step you were meant to take. What initially feels like an obstacle might, in truth, be a divine redirection.

Life happens *for* us, not *to* us. There is always a reason for the signs that appear. When you encounter them, take a deep breath and tune in to your inner guidance. Ask yourself: *What is the lesson here?* Look at the synchronicities that have unfolded in your life today and appreciate them. Be grateful for them—even if you find the situation inconvenient or annoying—because there may be a deeper purpose nudging you to awaken, notice, or grow.

Stay present to your experiences. Pay attention to what unfolds, because everything—whether it stops you in your tracks or encourages you to move forward—is happening *for* you. Each sign is an invitation to step more fully into what you are called to do.

There Are No Coincidences

*"Don't dismiss the synchronicity of what is happening right now finding its way into your life at just this moment.'
There are no coincidences in the universe, only convergences of will, intent, and experience."*

~ Neale Donald Walsch

People and opportunities often arrive precisely when we need them. We may not believe the timing is right—yet it always is. The key is paying attention to what is happening in the present moment. Whatever we are willing or intending for ourselves, we will eventually experience.

The timing, however, is rarely what we imagine to be important or ideal. Instead, it unfolds according to *Divine Timing*. It is natural to wish events would align with our own schedules—who doesn't? But the truth is that Divine Timing prevails. We don't know what we don't know. Some things we are aware we do not yet understand, and others remain completely outside our awareness.

The Universe—God, Source, however we name It—sees the larger picture. What appears to us as a delay or detour may, in fact, be perfect alignment within the grand design.

"When you live your life with an appreciation of coincidences and their meanings, you connect with the underlying field of infinite possibilities."
—Deepak Chopra

When you begin to notice and appreciate synchronicities—the countless alignments and sequences of events that must occur for us to have a particular experience—it can be transformative. It is never just one thing. Each step you take creates an impact—a ripple effect that influences everyone and everything around you.

Stay attuned to these synchronicities, and be grateful for the experiences they bring. Appreciate the so-called coincidences the Universe provides. Recognize that many of the opportunities and blessings that develop and unfold for us truly are created by God. Place your mind in gratitude and thankfulness, and stay aware of everything that had to converge for you to be right here, right now.

Know this: there are no coincidences. The reason you are reading these words is because you were meant to read them—right here, right now.

Make a Commitment

"Commitment is what transforms a promise into a reality...
Commitment is the stuff character is made of; the power to
change the face of things. It is the daily triumph of
integrity over skepticism."

~ Abraham Lincoln

For me, commitment looks like this: In 2006, I dedicated myself to training and certifying coaches. Today, in 2024, I remain steadfast in that commitment.

Now ask yourself: *What am I committed to? What ignites my passion? What do I want to contribute to the world? How do I want to be remembered?*

Have you solidified your commitment in writing? Shared it with someone you trust? Taken tangible steps toward fulfilling it? Do you have a clear, well-structured plan?

Commitment is powerful—but even more crucial is following through. Aligning your actions with your words is paramount, as we've already discussed. Whatever you commit to, backing it up with consistent action is essential. Ideally, your commitment should align with your passion—something that excites you, endures over time, and resonates deeply within you.

My hope for you is twofold: first, that you have identified what you are meant to contribute to the world; and second, that you have made a resolute commitment to share it. Just as importantly, I hope you have begun outlining a concrete plan to bring that commitment to life.

If you are still searching for that defining commitment—that passion waiting to be shared—I invite you to consider hiring a coach. Coaching offers unique insights into your deepest desires. You will experience the power of accountability and step into a supportive relationship where you can commit to your dream with confidence.

The Law of Consistency

"Motivation gets you going, but discipline keeps you growing. That's the Law of consistency. It doesn't matter how talented you are; it doesn't matter how many opportunities you receive. If you want to grow, consistency is the key. Small disciplines repeated with consistency every day lead to great achievements gained slowly over time."

~ John C. Maxwell

I like to think I lead by example when it comes to consistency. For instance, I have been faithfully recording and releasing my podcast, *The Power of Now: A Guide to Spiritual Enlightenment with Gilda and Barbara.* We've released more than 260 episodes—and every week, a new one goes live. That is consistency: showing up, getting it done, and doing the work.

It's time-consuming. There's no financial compensation for it at this stage. It is, instead, an act of love—a way of giving back to the universe for all the gifts we've received.

My hope is that listeners receive something of value—a word that resonates, a message that stirs the heart, or even just the reminder that showing up consistently, even without immediate results, is itself a sacred offering. Each episode is my way of saying: *Thank you for the blessings, joys, and wonders I have received. Now I give back.*

I love the Law of Consistency because John Maxwell is right: if you keep showing up and doing something again and again, you grow. You gain experience. You get better. You gain confidence. Your message becomes clearer, your delivery stronger, and your gift to the world brighter.

So, reflect for a moment: *What could you be doing consistently to make a difference in the world?* Whatever it is, commit to it. Shine your light. Lead the way. Be your best.

Response Ability

"It's easy to dodge our responsibilities, but we cannot dodge the consequences of dodging our responsibilities."

~ Josiah Stamp

We must follow through on the responsibilities we've taken on. If we don't, there will be consequences. Sometimes the cost is subtle: letting yourself down, losing integrity, weakening your word, forfeiting trust, or missing opportunities for wealth, love, peace, and harmony—all because you avoided a responsibility or broke a commitment you once made.

It is essential to follow through with what you say you will do so that your word carries weight. When your words and actions align, people know they can trust and rely on you. When you speak, they will pay attention and take you seriously. That is personal integrity—being true.

Take an honest look at your life. Are there things you've neglected—responsibilities that are yours but remain unfinished? If so, it may be time to make amends and take care of that lingering business. It is always better to face what you have been putting off—whether from procrastination or avoidance—when you know it is yours to handle.

Avoid the cost of dodging responsibility. Show up.

Show up for yourself.

Show up for others when you have committed to them.

And above all, show up for God—so that God can show up for you in miraculous ways.

Letting Go of Resentment

"Resentment is like drinking poison and then hoping it will kill your enemies."

~ Nelson Mandela

"When you hold resentment toward another, you are bound to that person or condition by an emotional link that is stronger than steel. Forgiveness is the only way to dissolve that link and get free."

~ Catherine Ponder

These two quotations capture the essence of resentment with striking clarity. Nelson Mandela's words remind us that resentment harms not the person it is aimed at, but the one who carries it. It is self-inflicted suffering—mental, spiritual, and even physical.

Catherine Ponder deepens this truth by describing resentment as an emotional bond "stronger than steel," binding us to the very people or situations we most wish to escape. The only way to dissolve that bond is through forgiveness. When we forgive, the emotional link dissolves, and we regain our freedom.

Together, Mandela and Ponder illuminate both the heavy cost of resentment and the liberating power of forgiveness. Holding on to resentment hinders our own well-being, burdening us with stress, tension, and negativity. Choosing forgiveness—though sometimes difficult—is an act of release, a gift we give ourselves.

I encourage you to practice forgiveness. Release the resentment you may hold toward people, situations, or even circumstances beyond your control. In doing so, you choose peace and well-being over poison. Let go, trust the process, and allow yourself to find inner peace.

Forgiveness Brings Peace

"God is bigger than time, dates, and appointments. He wants you to move through this day with a quiet heart, an inward assurance that He is in control, a peaceful certainty that your life is in His hands, a deep trust in His plan and purposes, and a thankful disposition toward all that He allows. He wants you to put your faith in Him, not in a timetable. He wants you to wait on Him and wait for Him. In his perfect way, He will put everything together, see to every detail, arrange every circumstance, and order every step to bring to pass what He has for you."

~ Roy Lessin

This quotation is a powerful reminder that God is for us, not against us. He wants us to demonstrate His glory, to show up for Him, to live in peace because of Him, and to know in our hearts that we can trust He will show up for us in divine and perfect timing.

We often say hindsight is 20/20. Looking back, it's easy to see how certain events shaped our path. You may realize, *If that hadn't happened, I wouldn't be where I am today.* Those experiences—pleasant or painful—helped you grow stronger, wiser, and more resilient. They shaped you into the person you are now.

I know there have been times in my own life when I was sad, depressed, hurt, even baffled—wondering, *How could someone do that to me?* And yet, those very moments molded me into who I am today. How could we ever develop true compassion if we had never walked through hardship ourselves? We may never fully know what another person is experiencing, but similar struggles give us the capacity to empathize more deeply and to extend compassion when and where it's needed most.

There's a saying: *Hurt people hurt people.* More often than not, cruelty is learned. Those who lash out are often carrying their own wounds, inflicted by someone else's pain.

The question is—have you been able to forgive the person who caused you pain, anxiety, or stress? Sometimes we'll never know why someone acted out of anger or meanness. But here's what I do know: forgiveness is freedom. When we forgive, we step into a new lightness, a new peace, a new freedom that releases us from the weight of bitterness.

So I encourage you—move toward forgiveness. Release those who hurt you, not because what they did was right, but because you deserve to be free. When you forgive, you loosen the grip of the past and open yourself to the peace God wants for you.

Acceptance ~ The Key to Serenity

"When you are sorrowful, look again in your heart, and you shall see that in truth you are weeping for that which has been your delight."

~ Khalil Gibran

"Don't cry because it's over. Smile because it happened."

~ Dr. Seuss

Sorrow, grieving, letting go . . . In life, change and loss are inevitable. When they arrive, we must become still and adjust to a new reality. Losing someone precious is deeply painful. Conversely, meeting someone new—someone who shares our values and vision—can feel like falling in love.

This is the rhythm of our human experience: what goes up must come down. Elation and joy are often followed by their opposites. We live in a world of duality—night and day, dark and light. To find true peace of heart and mind, we must seek balance. And balance, I believe, comes from living heart-centered and, more specifically, present in the moment.

When you are present, you are here now. If your mind dwells on the past, you may feel sorrow or joy depending on what once was. If your thoughts rush ahead to the future, you may feel fear of the unknown. But when your mind rests fully in the present, focused on this moment, you will discover inner peace.

There is joy in simply knowing that you are here—that you have made it through to the other side of sorrow. Choosing gratitude, even in difficult situations, can shift your energy and offer comfort in times of grief. Whether you are mourning the loss of a loved one or a cherished animal companion, you can honor the blessing of that experience and, with gentleness, let go. In doing so, you open yourself to the possibility of the new and amazing experiences the Universe still has in store for you.

Every experience, whether marked by trauma or joy, adds depth to your being. Life's challenges may have deepened your compassion, equipping you to walk alongside others facing their own trials. Perhaps your journey has given you the ability to provide value as you share your wisdom, solace, and hope—to remind them that healing is possible, and that happiness can and will return.

Trust the Universe ~ Eliminate Fear

"Fatigue makes fools of us all; it robs us of our skill, our judgment, and blinds us to creative solutions."
~ Harvey McKay

When we lack sleep, we become so fatigued that we cannot tune in or access our higher consciousness—the place where we receive those intuitive, almost magical answers that provide the perfect solutions to the challenges we face.

"Our fatigue is often caused not by work but by worry, frustration, and resentment."
~ Dale Carnegie

When we worry, what is that worry really about? It's about the future. We fear what might happen and become consumed by *what ifs*. Yet worry accomplishes little. Whatever is going to happen will happen. It is wise to take proactive steps to align your actions with the outcomes you desire, but there is also something essential called trust.

Trust the Universe instead of fretting over what may never occur. Trust your intuition and allow it to guide you. When you take inspired steps based on that guidance, you can move forward with confidence, knowing that your path—because it aligns with your inner wisdom—is exactly where you need to be. You don't need to worry, because you have tuned in and connected, receiving the right answers for yourself. They may not be the right answers for someone else, and if you share your path, others might not support it. I've certainly encountered people who tried to discourage me from pursuing certain steps, but I said, *No, this is it.* Even if it doesn't turn out perfectly, I learn along the way, and this is my path—the lesson I am meant to learn in this moment.

So don't worry; be happy. Let your inner guidance show you the way. Trust your inner guidance, and then you have nothing to worry about. Frustration often arises from resistance—resistance to what is. As mentioned previously, resentment is like carrying unnecessary baggage, akin to taking poison and hoping someone else will suffer instead. None of these emotions serve you.

Instead, let go of worry, frustration, and resentment. Tune in to your higher self and your inner guidance. Trust that guidance, follow your intuition, take baby steps—so it's not too far outside your comfort zone—and relax as you allow yourself to be amazed at the way the Universe unfolds everything perfectly, just for you.

Divine Grace

"There but for the grace of God go I."
~ John Bradford

This timeless phrase reminds us not to judge others. When we find ourselves tempted to judge, we must remember that we could just as easily be in the same situation. That is the heart of Bradford's words: *There but for the grace of God go I.* We all live under God's divine grace, and because of that, we are blessed.

"Divine grace is the divine influence that operates in humans to regenerate and sanctify, to inspire virtuous impulses, and to impart strength to endure trials and resist temptation."
~ Oxford English Dictionary

I believe we are all given divine grace—if we ask for it. Sometimes, we simply need to ask for what we need.

The truth is, we are surrounded by blessings. Acknowledge the grace that is yours, and give thanks for it. If you catch yourself judging someone else, pause and remember: *That could be me.* Be grateful for where you are today, for the blessings that already fill your life.

And when you face trials and tribulations—as we all do— hold fast. When you make it through to the other side, remember to be grateful and give thanks for the grace that carried you through.

Divine Timing

"Patience is power. Patience is not an absence of action; rather it is "timing". It waits on the right time to act, for the right principles and in the right way."

~ Fulton J. Sheen

Patience requires humility. It also requires the wisdom to understand that things don't always happen when we want them to. Sometimes we have to wait—and often, the waiting brings results far greater than we could have imagined.

I believe patience is essential. It isn't our timing that matters most—it's God's timing. When God is ready to bless you, that's when it will happen. I know the feeling of wanting things to unfold immediately, believing life would be easier if everything happened now. But that isn't how God works. God sees the entire picture; we don't. He knows exactly when the timing is perfect for us to receive what we've been asking for.

That doesn't mean we stop acting. Far from it. We keep taking small steps forward, moving in the direction of our calling. The whole picture may never be revealed to us—or it may only come into focus later—but either way, it unfolds in God's timing. Part of our work is learning to wait for the right moment, tuning in to our intuition to discern, *Is this the right time for me to move forward?* When the answer is yes, we move not only with purpose but also for the right reasons, grounded in principles that matter.

We move forward not just for ourselves but to give back—to uplift those less fortunate or those who may not yet feel the same connection to the Divine. By demonstrating patience, we set an example for others, helping them learn to wait for the right guidance that will illuminate their own path.

As I've said before, we are all born with divine gifts meant to be shared with the world. I believe with all my heart that we incarnated to bring forth something unique within us— something only we can offer. So even if the timing doesn't look perfect, even if things aren't unfolding according to our plans, remember this: God's vision is greater than ours. His plans are larger, fuller, and always for our good.

Show up. Share your gifts in this present moment. And trust that when you do, God will show up for you—in miraculous ways.

Laughter ~ Unifying, Healing and Sacred

"Laughter is a holy thing. It is as sacred as music and silence and solemnity, maybe more sacred. Laughter is like a prayer, like a bridge over which creatures tiptoe to meet each other. Laughter is like mercy; it heals. When you can laugh at yourself, you are free."

~ Ted Loder

I love this quotation because it reminds me of the sacred power of laughter. It lifts the heart, raises the spirit, and carries us closer to the presence of the Divine. When I first began connecting with my spiritual guides, I discovered that laughter was a key that unlocked the door. After a few deep breaths, I would find myself joyously laughing until laughter lifted my vibration to the frequency where I could easily receive their guidance. Over time, I learned to reach that same meditative, receptive state simply by taking three deep breaths in and out. After the third breath, the connection arrives—delicious and undeniable.

Laughter is a healer. As Ted Loder so beautifully said, it is sacred. It uplifts us, unites us, and reminds us of the goodness in life. True laughter never wounds; it does not come at the expense of another's dignity. Derisive insults disguised as "jokes" are not funny. They cut rather than heal, and they are never acceptable.

But the kind of laughter that arises from joy—the kind that bubbles up when life surprises us with its grace, when we share a moment of delight with a loved one, when we simply allow ourselves to feel light again—that laughter is holy. It cheers us on, connects us to one another, and opens us to the presence of Spirit.

May your laughter ripple outward—healing, connecting, and reminding the world that joy itself is a prayer.

Laughter ~ Vibration and Frequency

In both spiritual and scientific contexts, laughter is often described as raising your vibration—or shifting your state. Modern research affirms what ancient wisdom has long suggested: laughter transforms us.

From a scientific view:

- **Neurochemistry:** Laughter triggers endorphins, dopamine, and serotonin—the "feel-good" chemicals that elevate mood.
- **Stress reduction:** It lowers cortisol, the body's primary stress hormone.
- **Heart and breath rhythm:** Genuine laughter increases oxygen intake and harmonizes heart rate variability.
- **Social bonding:** Shared laughter strengthens connection, reducing feelings of isolation and anxiety.

Together, these shifts create a healthier internal state—what many call a "higher frequency."

From a spiritual view:

Many traditions describe emotions as carrying vibrational frequencies:

- **Low vibration:** fear, anger, guilt, shame.
- **High vibration:** love, joy, gratitude, laughter.

Laughter is seen as one of the fastest ways to raise energy, break stagnant patterns, and align with openness, love, and joy.

A practical way to think of it: laughter acts as an instant reset button. It shifts you out of heaviness into lightness—physically, emotionally, and energetically.

Remarkably, physiology doesn't distinguish between genuine and intentional laughter; both trigger endorphins and reduce stress hormones. Practiced daily, laughter conditions your body and spirit to move quickly into a lighter, higher vibration.

Your Creative, Conscious Mind

"Most of the so-called bad things that happen in people's lives are due to unconsciousness. They are self-created, or rather, ego-created dramas. When you are fully conscious, drama does not come into your life anymore."

~ Eckhart Tolle

Eckhart Tolle experienced a profound spiritual transformation at the age of twenty-nine. His insights are invaluable, especially as you embark on your journey toward greatness and the sharing of your light with the world.

Drama can be a significant hindrance as you work to fulfill your potential. Tolle reminds us that the antidote to drama is consciousness. When we become fully aware, we step out of ego-driven patterns and into alignment with our Divine purpose. Bruce Lipton echoes this with his teaching on "keeping the honeymoon alive." He explains that when we operate from the creative, conscious mind, we align ourselves with our chosen path. In that state, drama fades into the background and harmony takes its place.

By contrast, slipping into the subconscious—or living on autopilot—triggers thoughts and behaviors misaligned with our true selves. This is why it is essential to remain present, to observe our thoughts, and to choose consciously. Operating from a creative, aware state empowers us to live in integrity with our deepest purpose.

Remember: when you shine your light and lead by example, you inspire others to do the same. And when you show up for God, you invite the miraculous into your life.

Surround Yourself with Positive People

*"As you evolve you will make a lot of people uncomfortable.
Evolve anyway."*

~ Author unknown

I once came across an image online of a person sitting in the lotus position with the words, *"As you evolve, you will make a lot of people uncomfortable. Evolve anyway."* That message struck me deeply because it rings so true. As we grow spiritually, we naturally evolve. I believe our auric field begins to shine more brightly, and people notice. Many are drawn to the light we emanate and want to know more. Yet for those who are not ready—or who have not yet reached a place of openness in their own journey—being around such light can make them feel uncomfortable.

When I first began growing spiritually, I noticed that some people seemed uneasy in my presence. I understood why: I was happy—radiating positive energy wherever I went, living in the present moment. Often people would ask, "Why are you happy all the time?" For those stuck in ego or weighed down by dissatisfaction, witnessing someone else's joy can feel unsettling. And yet, as the quote reminds us: evolve anyway.

As you continue to shine your light brightly, you may also awaken something in others—especially those having a difficult day or struggling with their outlook. Your example can remind them that change is possible, that gratitude shifts perspective, and that there is always something to appreciate in each day.

The lesson here is to surround yourself with people who share your wavelength, your energy, and your path. When you do, you won't encounter resistance. Instead, you'll find the encouragement, inspiration, and support to show up authentically and to radiate brilliantly the life force expanding within you.

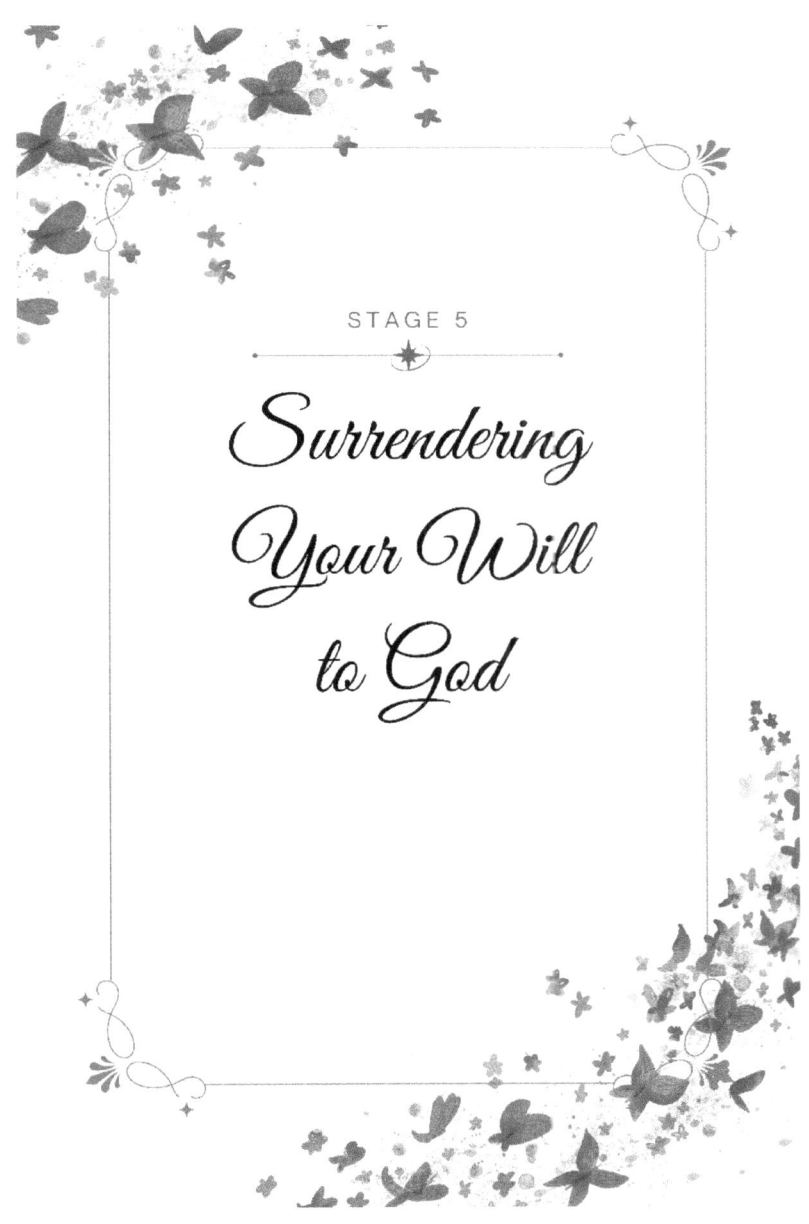

STAGE 5

Surrendering Your Will to God

You Are a Creator

This stage begins with the recognition that you are a creator—and then comes the deeper questioning: What does God want me to do? What is my purpose? Why am I here? What is my passion?

It is the point at which you come to believe in a Higher Power, begin to recognize evidence of that power at work in your life, and choose to surrender your own will to something greater. This surrender is not about giving up or losing control; it is about entrusting your life to God's wisdom and aligning yourself with God's wishes.

When you reach this stage, you acknowledge that your path is not meant to be directed solely by ego or personal desire. Instead, you turn your will and your life over to God, trusting that divine guidance will lead you toward your true purpose.

Indecision, Doubt, and Fear

Will publishing this book make a difference in the world? I ask myself that question often. I have my doubts, too. Should I continue writing this book to encourage people to show up for God?

"Indecision, doubt, and fear—the members of this Unholy Trio—are closely related. Where one is found, the other two are close at hand."
~ Napoleon Hill

Indecision: there it is. I catch myself doubting. I don't necessarily feel afraid—at least not in the obvious sense—but perhaps there's a subtle fear of wasting my time. Or maybe not. Still, as Hill reminds us, fear, doubt, and indecision are often intertwined.

"I learned that courage was not the absence of fear, but the triumph over it. The brave man is not the one who does not feel afraid, but he who conquers that fear."
~ Nelson Mandela

I've heard from people who tell me they enjoy my messages, that my words resonate. I treasure that feedback because when you're writing a book, you can't always see the impact. You don't know if your words will make a difference. And the doubts creep in: Is this something I should be doing? Should I continue?

Here's what I've learned: when doubt arises, the best place to turn is to Higher Guidance. That's what I do—even when feedback is scarce. I check in with my inner knowing and ask: Is this what I'm called to do? Is this what I'm meant to do? And each time, I hear the same answer: yes. I believe I'm meant to encourage others to show up for God—so God can show up for them in miraculous ways.

I also believe we are all born with a Divine Purpose. It lives within us, waiting to be expressed. It is the gift we are meant to give back to the world. So if you find yourself on the fence—in indecision, doubting your worth, wondering if your message matters—don't shelve it. Don't stop. Those nudges would not have come to you if they weren't meant to be expressed and shared.

Step out of your own way and deliver your message, whatever it may be, because someone needs to hear it. There may be thousands of voices speaking similar truths, but the way you say it may be the way someone else needs to hear it.

So today I encourage you: if you are wrestling with indecision, doubt, or fear, set them aside. Move forward—full steam ahead—and do what you are called to do.

Finding Your Unique Gifts

"The goal in life is not to attain some imaginary ideal; it is to find and fully use our own gifts."

~ Gay Hendricks

Gay Hendricks, the author of *The Big Leap: Conquer Your Hidden Fear and Take Life to the Next Level*, has written extensively with his wife on living with authenticity and purpose. This quote captures one of his core teachings: that our highest calling is not to conform to external expectations but to uncover and embody our unique gifts.

It is vital that we resist living according to someone else's script. Don't listen to the voices that insist, "You have to do this," or "You should do that." Each of us carries within us a divine gift meant to be shared with the world. Only you can discover yours, and only you can allow it to flow from your spirit into expression.

If you haven't yet discovered your divine gift, I encourage you to begin with exploration. Follow your curiosity. Try new experiences. Ask yourself: What am I drawn to? What have I always wanted to try? It could be anything! Perhaps it's something physical, like sailing across open water, surfing waves, or climbing mountains. Maybe it's standing at the summit, looking out over the world, when inspiration strikes and you realize: *This is where I feel alive. This is where I am most connected to Source, most energized, most inspired.* That sense of connection is love waiting to flow through you.

For others, inspiration may come through art, film, music, or storytelling. It may be sparked while walking through a museum, sitting in a theater, or even watching a single scene that stirs something within you. Creativity takes countless forms, and when you tune in to what longs to be expressed through you, you will recognize your divine gift.

As Hendricks reminds us, "It's not about attaining some imaginary ideal." Too often we are raised to chase ideals that may not reflect our true path. A woman, for example, may be pressured to have children, yet that is not the right path for everyone—and that is perfectly okay. What matters is listening to your heart. Where is your creativity guiding you? How can you allow it to flow outward, not just for yourself but as a gift to the world?

The Answers Are Within You

"Some men have thousands of reasons why they cannot do what they want to do when all they need is one reason why they can."

~ Martha Graham

Are you making excuses for why you can't move forward? Are you avoiding responsibility for what you know you need to do? Or are you caught in confusion, uncertain about your next best step?

Confusion is often just another form of resistance. If you feel genuinely unclear, there are simple ways to move through it. Pray for guidance. Ask a trusted mentor for perspective. Hire a coach to help you find clarity, or a consultant to suggest next steps. Support is available—but ultimately, the question *What is my next best step?* can only be answered from within you.

What gifts are you being called to create and share with the world? My belief is this: if an idea has been entrusted to you by God, the Universe, or your Higher Power, it is because you are meant to take action to manifest it. Overwhelm and doubt are natural, but they are not signs for you to give up. If you are called to create, it is because you have been chosen to do so. The gift is yours to develop and deliver Take action. Work with a coach, consultant, or mentor to help you get started with your mission. Pray and meditate on it. But most of all— begin.

"A deep-seated state of fear, need, lack, and incompleteness is part of the human condition in its unredeemed and unenlightened state. In an enlightened state, the individual possesses a profound clarity of vision and understanding, allowing them to navigate life's complexities with heightened awareness."
~ Eckhart Tolle

In an enlightened state, we *know*. We know what to do, the words to speak, the path to follow. We know our next best step. We act from clarity, and in doing so, we authentically shine our light.

One of my deepest callings is to channel as much light as I can and to share it with you. My hope is that as you read these words, you will tap into that same light—allowing it to inspire you, strengthen you, and guide you into the work you are called to do. Do not let excuses hold you back. Go for it, and you will be astonished at how the doors open. God always makes a way. As I often say: *Show up for God, and God will show up for you—in miraculous ways.*

Discovering Your Divine Purpose

"When you want something; all the universe conspires in helping you to achieve it."

~ Paul Coelho

I believe we are all born with gifts meant to be shared with the world. Paulo Coelho said, *"When you want something, the Universe conspires on your behalf to help you achieve it."* That's a beautiful truth, but it raises an important question: How do you uncover your Divine Purpose so the Universe can assist you in fulfilling it?

Discovering your Divine Purpose looks different for everyone, because each of us is a unique and beautiful spiritual being. The journey to reveal your divine gifts and find your purpose may be a lifelong pursuit—or it may unfold quickly. My own journey lasted a decade.

I had a persistent knowing that I was meant to do something other than develop software, which had been my career for many years. I immersed myself in reading, attending seminars and workshops, and practicing various spiritual disciplines. I researched extensively before finally realizing that teaching people how to coach was my gift. Out of that discovery, I designed and developed a coaching system that has since proven to be effective. Creating that system remains one of my greatest contributions to the world.

If you are seeking your Divine Purpose, here are a few practices that may help:

Meditation. Quieting your mind allows you to connect with your inner being, where the essence of who you truly are resides. If meditation is new to you, be patient—it may take time to master the spiritual practice of calming your mind.

Journaling. Writing down your thoughts and feelings can bring clarity to what matters most. Journaling also provides a way to look back on your experiences, recognize patterns and progress, and reflect on how your values, strengths, and passions have evolved over time.

Self-reflection. Pause and take a deep breath. Contemplate the things that bring you joy. Ask yourself: What comes naturally to me? What am I truly passionate about? If I had unlimited time and resources, what would I create or pursue? You may find that your deepest passions lie in the activities that delighted you as a child.

Guidance. Consider working with a spiritual or career coach who can help you explore your purpose while offering motivation, support, and encouragement. As you navigate this inner journey, a spiritual coach can also help you strengthen your intuition.

Synchronicities. Pay attention to meaningful coincidences, signs, and symbols that cross your path—these often serve as guideposts, pointing you toward your purpose.

I hope some of these ideas spark something within you, helping you gain insights into your true passion and purpose.

Remember, discovering your Divine Purpose is not a one-time event but a lifelong journey of self-discovery that unfolds over time. Your purpose may evolve as you grow, and that is part of the process. Be patient with yourself. Trust your intuition. Stay open—because you never know what the

Universe has in store for you. Many gifts may be coming your way.

Your Divine Gifts are Valuable

"We are all born with divine gifts that we are meant to share with the world. Shine your Light and lead the way for others."

~ Barbara Wainwright

"You are so part of the world that your slightest action contributes to its reality. Your breath changes the atmosphere. Your encounters with others alter the fabrics of their lives, and the lives of those who come in contact with them."

~ Jane Roberts

It is essential to acknowledge your impact on the world. Accept this truth and move forward, bringing your full presence into each moment. When you show up fully—aware, intentional, and spiritually grounded—you naturally create a positive ripple that uplifts humanity.

I believe that each of us is born with a divine purpose that makes us uniquely valuable; our innate gifts are divinely inspired, and we are meant to share them with the world.

Your gifts deserve your acknowledgment and acceptance. Say to yourself, *Yes, I am divinely inspired, and I do have gifts that can serve the world.* Then, once you have embraced that truth, begin taking small, deliberate steps to bring those gifts into form, manifesting them to make the world a better place for everyone.

Your offering does not need to be extravagant. Sometimes the simplest acts carry the most power. A smile, for example, can be a profound gift—acknowledging another person's presence, affirming their worth, and reminding them they are seen. That single moment of connection may be exactly what they needed.

Believe In Yourself

"You are never given a dream without also being given the power to make it come true. You may have to work for it, however." ~ Richard Bach

"Don't believe what your eyes are telling you. All they show is limitation. Look with your understanding. Find out what you already know and you will see the way to fly."

~ Richard Bach

Richard Bach, in his book *Illusions: The Adventures of a Reluctant Messiah*, reminds us of a profound truth: You are never given a dream without also being given the power to make it come true. Yes, it may require effort, dedication, and perseverance—but the very fact that the dream was placed in your heart means you already carry within you the capacity to fulfill it. Please have the confidence to move forward with your dream wholeheartedly.

When Bach cautions us not to trust only what our eyes reveal but to "look with your understanding," I believe he is pointing us to look within our hearts—through our spiritual being. If you are inspired by a dream or a belief, there's a reason for that. Dreams and inspirations are not random; they are divine invitations. If God, Spirit, or the Universe has impressed an idea upon you, then the resources, mentors, tools, and opportunities you need to manifest it will also be provided. The dream and the means to achieve it are inseparable gifts.

I remember when someone once told me I would speak in front of thousands of people. At the time, the thought terrified me. I had never done any public speaking, and even the idea of standing on a stage made me want to retreat. Today, while I have not yet spoken to an audience of thousands, I have spoken to groups far larger than I once imagined possible. More importantly, I have learned to step forward with faith, showing up for God, listening to my intuition, and trusting the inner guidance that calls me to share my beliefs about the connection between our Creator and each one of us.

I like to think of each of us as a drop of water in the vast ocean of collective consciousness. That ocean represents the shared energy, wisdom, and creativity available to us all. Each drop carries its own unique vibration, filtered through individual perception and experience. The invitation is for you to discern what resonates for you: What is your truth? What sparks your passion? What lights you up and makes your heart sing?

Take a moment today to quiet yourself and listen. Let your heart speak. What does the love energy within you want to express? Perhaps it is as simple as offering a smile to someone you pass in the hallway or taking a moment to speak a kind word to someone. These may seem like small gestures, but they are profound when they come from the heart.

Follow your heart today. The dream within you is not an accident. It was given to you for a reason—because you are meant to bring it into the world.

Sometimes "Good Enough" is a Thing

"I'm never pleased with anything, I'm a perfectionist, it's part of who I am."

~ Michael Jackson

"Have no fear of perfection - you'll never reach it."

~ Salvador Dali

"Perfection is not attainable, but if we chase perfection we can catch excellence."

~ Vince Lombardi

Many people are held back by perfectionism. If that resonates with you, I want to encourage you to keep moving forward. You don't need to be perfect. In fact, whatever you are doing doesn't have to be perfect. It may turn out to be exactly what someone needs—whether it's your words, your presence, or your work.

Michael Jackson once admitted, "I'm never pleased with anything. I'm a perfectionist; it's part of who I am." Can you imagine that? Of course, he wanted everything to be just right. But the truth is, *perfect* is only an opinion—someone's perspective on what is ideal. Don't let yourself be driven or paralyzed by another person's, or even your own, perception of perfection.

Dalí offered wise counsel when he said, "Have no fear of perfection. You'll never reach it." That makes sense, doesn't it? If perfection is subjective and unreachable, why let it stop you? Persevere anyway.

And then there's Vince Lombardi, the legendary football coach who led his teams to multiple championships: "Perfection is not attainable, but if we chase perfection, we can catch excellence." His words remind us that striving can elevate us, even if perfection itself remains out of reach.

So here's my encouragement: Don't wait for everything to be perfect before pursuing your passion, serving others, or shining your light. Don't wait for all the pieces to align just so—because chances are it may never happen in the way you imagine. Take action anyway.

Let me share a story from my own life. For years, I believed everything had to be perfect, and that belief held me back. When my daughter was six, I was brushing her hair one morning, fussing with every strand, determined to make her ponytail flawless. Suddenly she pulled away, looked at me, and said, "That's good enough, Mom!" *Good enough.* In that moment I realized something powerful: good enough is a thing. You don't have to reach perfection. Sometimes *good enough* truly is enough.

Perfectionism often grows out of our own harsh self-criticism. But here's the truth: you don't need perfection to make an impact. And if you aspire to be a life coach, please hear this— your life doesn't need to be perfect either. Coaching isn't about having a flawless life; it's about supporting your clients as they create inspired, purposeful lives of their own.

Your Spiritual Guidance System

"The main reason intuition is so important is this: It's a clear sign that you're connecting with your inner spiritual guidance system. Intuition is a direct signal from your deepest self that you are navigating from your true center."

~ Gay Hendricks

I believe it is essential for each of us to navigate from our true center. What is your divine purpose? By tapping into intuition, we can ensure that we are on the right path, working with the right people, and taking the right steps.

So today, I extend this encouragement to you: show up. Show up consistently. Approach the practice of tuning into your inner guidance with a positive attitude, knowing that your commitment will yield meaningful outcomes. When you do, you will begin to receive valuable insights that illuminate your next steps and allow your journey to unfold with greater ease.

As you practice following your intuition, you'll grow more confident in its wisdom. With time, you'll recognize it as a reliable compass—one that aligns your plans and actions with your divine path.

Develop Your Intuition

"Showing up is essential. Showing up consistently is powerful. Showing up consistently with a positive outlook is even more powerful."

~ Jeff Olson

Jeff Olson's words remind me of my early days of developing intuition. I realized it was crucial to set appointments—not with others, but with myself. These were sacred appointments to show up for my intuition, my inner guidance.

This dedicated time allowed me to nurture my intuitive abilities. I created an environment conducive to stillness and meditation: scented candles, essential oils, and incense to awaken my senses; quartz crystals to enhance my energy field; and soft meditation music to soothe my soul. This was my way of showing up for God—so that God could show up for me in miraculous ways. By establishing a consistent routine, I created space to connect with my spiritual guides. Approaching this practice with a positive outlook helped me tap into higher guidance and inner wisdom, enabling me to make better decisions and take purposeful steps forward.

One of the most effective ways to develop intuition is to cultivate mindfulness and self-awareness. Practices such as meditation, journaling, or simply pausing for moments of quiet reflection help you tune into your inner thoughts and feelings. Over time, you'll begin to recognize and trust your intuitive signals. Asking for confirmation can strengthen that trust, ensuring you have confidence in the guidance you receive. Developing your intuitive prowess is important as part of your spiritual journey.

Your body can also serve as a powerful compass. Physical sensations often reveal intuitive truths before your mind does. Think of the butterflies you feel when something excites you or the discomfort that signals misalignment. Sometimes there's an unmistakable yes in your body—the sense of "This is it!"—when you're considering your options. Try asking yourself questions such as "Is this the right step for me?" and pay attention to how your body responds. At first, the signals may feel unfamiliar or confusing, which is why it's important to check in frequently and ask for confirmation that you're on the right path.

Another valuable practice is intuitive decision-making. When faced with choices, try setting logic aside for a moment and simply tune into your gut feelings. What is the very first thought or feeling that arises? What sense do you get, even before you begin analyzing? Trusting your intuition in these moments can often lead to surprising insights, clarity, and outcomes.

Begin tuning in and developing your intuition, because that's your inner guidance system—the compass designed to help you move forward with confidence, even when the path feels new or uncertain. Most importantly, it will guide you toward your highest good—what you are truly meant to do.

The Misfits, the Rebels, the Troublemakers

"Here's to the crazy ones. The misfits. The rebels. The troublemakers. The round pegs in the square holes. The ones who see things differently."

~ Walter Isaacson

There have been times in my life when I felt like a crazy person—the one who takes risks, who does what others won't, the one who steps outside their comfort zone and does it anyway. Steve Jobs added to Isaacson's quote: "They're not fond of rules. You can quote them, disagree with them, glorify or vilify them, but the only thing you can't do is ignore them, because they change things."

Are you a change-maker? Are you ready to change the world? Is there something in your heart that keeps nagging at you? Do you feel like it's time—time to move forward, time to take action, time to get it done? Have you been putting it off? Have you been ignoring what your heart is telling you?

There can be consequences to ignoring those nudges. When you ignore what you are called to do, sometimes your body and mind will demand attention in other ways. The universe will get your attention—one way or another. That's why I strongly recommend: if you feel called to something, start moving forward today. It's okay to start with small steps. It is important to begin doing what you are meant to do. As Steve Jobs said, "The people who are the rebels, they push the human race forward, and while some people may see them as crazy, we see genius—because the ones who are crazy enough to think they can change the world are the ones who do."

If you have something inside that needs to be expressed in the world, start taking steps toward its creation so that you can live a fulfilled life. Know that the daring, seemingly crazy choices you make can, and will, truly make a difference. We are all born with divine gifts—everyone, without exception. These gifts are meant to be shared.

Consider this: if you don't step forward to share your gifts, someone else will. They will take the steps you've been holding back from taking. And one day, you might find yourself thinking, "Oh my goodness, that was supposed to be me. I was meant to be standing there. I was meant to share that message. I was meant to create that thing. I was meant to host that show. I was meant to live that dream, expressing my divine gifts in the world."

I encourage you to show up for God, so God can show up for you in miraculous ways. Don't doubt it for a second. This is the way the universe works. The universe responds when you demonstrate to the universe that you're willing to show up and do the work.

Pay Attention to the Nudges

"Destiny is not a matter of chance. It is a matter of choice.
It is not a thing to be waited for; it is a thing to be
achieved."

~ William Jennings Bryan

Is destiny a predetermined course of events? Perhaps. I've met people who said they waited years before discovering what they were truly called to do. Personally, I spent nearly a decade searching before realizing that my passion was coaching. Did I know then that I would one day teach thousands of people how to coach? Certainly not.

Discovering coaching as my destiny required more than soul-searching; it took research, exploration, and investment. I poured time and resources into learning various healing modalities, ways of connecting, and avenues of service. Each path taught me something valuable, but none compelled me to leap in fully—until I found coaching. I believe destiny is the work we are innately meant to do, the gift we are divinely inspired to share with the world. The question is: What within you is waiting to be uncovered?

Uncovering your destiny may require trial and error. You'll explore, test, and ask yourself: Is this the right place for me? Is this the training I need? Is this the path I'm meant to walk? Eventually, though, a breakthrough comes. And with it, the nudges.

By nudges, I mean the gentle but persistent inner prodding that pushes you toward your true calling. Just yesterday, one of my coaches shared how he kept feeling nudged to launch his coaching business. He had been sidetracked with other pursuits, but the sense of "You need to do this" kept returning.

Pay attention to those nudges. Notice the subtle signs guiding you forward. They are invitations to take the next step and begin offering your unique gift to the world. It may feel scary—stepping into something unfamiliar always does. Doubt may creep in: What if this isn't the right thing? But here's the truth: if it isn't, you'll find out quickly. And if you've been checking in with your intuition and receiving confirmation that it's the next right move, then it's time to jump in wholeheartedly. I know you will find it very rewarding.

Take the leap. Trust the nudge. See what unfolds.

Give Yourself Permission

"You never know when it is going to happen, when you will experience a moment that dramatically transforms your life. When you look back, often years later, you may see how a brief conversation or an insight you read somewhere, changed the entire course of your life."

~ Gay Henricks

I encourage you to follow your heart now and do what you are called to do. Trust your intuition, know you are on the right path, and give yourself permission to begin taking steps toward manifesting your divine gifts.

This quote comes from Gay Hendricks's book *Five Wishes: How One Simple Question Can Make Your Dreams Come True.*

I remember one such moment that changed the trajectory of my life. At the time, I was married—but it was an unusual marriage in that we never actually lived in the same house. How do you live that way and stay married? I was sitting in a therapist's office and said, "I feel like my husband is holding me back." The therapist gently replied, "Can you say, 'I'm letting him hold me back'?"

In an instant, my perspective shifted. I realized it had been my decision to remain in that relationship, my decision not to move on with my life. In that moment—just as Gay Hendricks described—I felt as though I had been given permission to follow my own truth. That single question empowered me to stop allowing my marriage to hold me back and to start pursuing my dreams, creating a life I truly loved.

My hope is that this book serves as that same kind of permission for you—to do or create what is in your heart to share with the world. Ask yourself: What difference do I want to make? What do I want to be remembered for? When I leave the room, what do I want people to say about me? Then give yourself permission to take action and make it happen.

In our coaching practice, we often ask clients, "What is it you truly want to create in the world?" We guide them to take a deep breath, focus on their inner being, and listen to what their heart reveals. From that sacred space, we craft a vision statement written as though their dream life already exists. When we deliver that vision statement to the client, it is often an emotional moment. Clients hear their deepest desires spoken aloud, perhaps for the first time, and see what life could look like if they allowed themselves to take steps toward what they're called to do—what is in their heart to create and experience. The vision statement is an affirmation. It becomes a powerful confirmation that they are indeed on the right path to a fulfilling life.

So I invite you: give yourself permission to take those steps you might not normally take. You are meant to manifest the glory of God within you. The dreams and desires in your heart are not there by accident. They are meant to be born into the world—through you.

Let yourself soar.

Stay Humble

"Stay hungry, stay young, stay foolish, stay curious, and, above all, stay humble, because just when you think you've got all the answers, that is the moment when some bitter twist of fate in the universe will remind you that you very much don't."

~ Tom Hiddleston

Staying humble is one of the greatest spiritual practices we can embrace. Humility keeps us grounded. It reminds us that every blessing, every gift, and every opportunity to serve are not solely of our own making but a result of collaboration with God, the Universe, and those who support and inspire us along the way.

Humility doesn't mean diminishing your worth or denying your accomplishments. Rather, it's about acknowledging your gifts with gratitude and choosing to use them in service of something greater than yourself. True humility is quiet confidence—an inner assurance of your value that frees you from the need to seek external validation or to measure yourself against others.

When we remain humble, we remain open. We remain teachable. We recognize that wisdom comes from many sources—our intuition, our mentors, our experiences, even our mistakes. Humility creates space for growth, allowing us to receive guidance more clearly and to connect more deeply with others.

As you walk your path of spiritual awakening—embracing miracles, following your intuition, and sharing your light— remember to walk with humility. Let gratitude be your constant companion, and let your actions speak louder than your words.

Humility also arises naturally as you evolve on your spiritual journey. Authentic spiritual teachers do not boast of their abilities. Instead, they embody peace and serenity, demonstrating by example the quiet strength of a humble heart.

Coming to Believe in Miracles

"God will make a way where there seems to be no way. He works in ways that we cannot see." ~ Don Moen

Miracles often appear when we least expect them. They simply happen—and when they do, I am amazed, stunned, and deeply moved all at once. Perhaps you feel the same when a miracle occurs in your life. Yet, at some level, we already know that God—the Universe—works in miraculous ways. So why are we still surprised? Maybe it's because part of us doubts we deserve the miracle—or perhaps part of us struggles to believe in miracles at all.

"With God, all things are possible." ~ Wayne Dyer

I have come to truly believe that all things are possible through God, through faith, and through divine guidance that shows up in miraculous ways. At the same time, I believe our own belief systems can become the very obstacles that prevent miracles from manifesting in our lives. When we commit to taking action as we are divinely instructed—to fulfill our destiny and our divine purpose—and when we trust the messages and nudges we are given, we begin to witness God working in miraculous ways. Because God is, and always will be, the worker of miracles.

"After witnessing miracles over a period of time, you begin to believe in them." ~ Barbara Wainwright

I live in gratitude for the ways God continues to reveal miracles, and I know that all we are asked to do is listen to our inner guidance and keep showing up.

Even when life doesn't appear to be coming together, if something arises from your soul—if it is divinely inspired—then it is meant to be expressed in the world. God will make a way. The path will be cleared, the doors will open, and miracles will unfold because you chose to show up for God.

Choose to See All Life as a Miracle ~ Because It Is

"Is suffering really necessary? Yes and no. If you had not suffered as you have, there would be no depth to you, no humility, and no compassion. Suffering cracks open the shell of ego, and then comes a point when it has served its purpose. Suffering is necessary until you realize it is unnecessary. True freedom and the end of suffering are living in such a way as if you had completely chosen whatever you feel or experience at this moment. This inner alignment with now is the end of suffering."

~ Eckhart Tolle

Acceptance is the key to serenity. When you accept what is—whatever is happening in the present moment—suffering ceases. In acceptance, you find peace.

When you see everything as a miracle, there is also no suffering. This is simply another way of being in acceptance. Acceptance does not mean you cannot change something if you don't like it; it means you remain at peace while navigating it. When you approach difficult situations from that place of peace, answers and solutions arise with grace. They feel like miracles—because miracles truly do happen when you believe in them.

You can choose to live as though everything is a miracle. And isn't life itself miraculous when you pause to reflect? The simple fact that you are here, alive, able to read this book, see it on your phone, or even hear it through audio—it's extraordinary when you consider the intricate technology working quietly behind the scenes to make it possible.

So today I encourage you: choose to see everything as a miracle. Accept what is unfolding in your life. Acknowledge it. Make peace with it. And if something isn't serving you, go within. Take a deep breath and ask: What is my next best step? What is the best solution to this uncomfortable situation? Trust the answers you receive, knowing they are exactly right for you.

That doesn't mean everyone will embrace your choices. Growth and alignment can sometimes unsettle those who have not yet discovered what is right for them. Still, your responsibility is not to ease their discomfort but to honor your own inner guidance. When you do, life reveals itself— moment by moment—as the miracle it has always been.

STAGE 6

Sharing Newfound Beliefs and Divine Gifts

Sharing Your Newfound Beliefs

The final stage unfolds once you are aligned with God's will. At this point, you are called to share your beliefs, breakthroughs, successes, commitment to God, and the gifts and grace you have received with others.

This act of sharing is a vital expression of your life's purpose. When you extend what has been given to you, you step fully into service. By shining your light and offering your divine gifts, you inspire others to awaken to their own. In this way, your journey of faith and transformation becomes a blessing far beyond yourself, creating ripples of grace that reach into the lives of others.

Fruit Is Good for You, But Love Is Better

"Look to what you have around you and be grateful, instead of searching for more. All you take with you when you leave this world is love, friendship, and good deeds."
~ Sylvia Browne

Sylvia Browne, a wise woman and prolific author, expressed a truth that continues to resonate with me. Her words remind us that material possessions are not what we carry beyond this life. What endures are the intangible treasures: love, friendship, and the positive impact of our good deeds.

"I've learned that people will forget what you said, people will forget what you did, but people will never forget how you made them feel."
~ Maya Angelou

Maya Angelou's insight echoes this sentiment. People may forget our words or even our actions, but they never forget how we made them feel. This universal truth underscores the enduring value of relationships and emotional connection.

In a world often consumed by consumerism, it is easy to lose sight of this reality. The pursuit of possessions rarely leads to lasting fulfillment. I once thought accumulating properties and material things would bring contentment, but in time I realized those gains fade. What truly remains are the connections we nurture and the lives we touch.

Take a moment to contemplate: What is the purpose of amassing material wealth if true abundance lies within us? Real wealth is measured in love, in friendships, and in the good we contribute to the world. It is about showing up for a higher purpose—for God—and leaving behind a legacy of kindness and compassion.

Reflect on the wisdom of Sylvia Browne and Maya Angelou, and embrace the truth that love, relationships, and good deeds hold immeasurable value. My daughter Emily, at just six years old, captured it beautifully when she said, "Fruit is good for you, but love is better."

Let us cherish these intangible riches, shine our light brightly, and lead the way for others.

Nurture Your Spiritual Growth

"When I genuinely love, I am extending myself, and when I am extending myself, I am growing. The more I love, the longer I love, the larger I become. Genuine love is self-replenishing. The more I nurture the spiritual growth of others, the more my own spiritual growth is nurtured."
~ M. Scott Peck

By now you know that I believe we are all born with divine gifts meant to be shared with the world. My encouragement to you is simple: share yours.

M. Scott Peck, in his classic book *The Road Less Traveled: A New Psychology of Love, Values, and Spiritual Growth*, wrote, "The more I nurture the spiritual growth in others, the more my own spiritual growth is nurtured." His words spoke deeply to me early in my journey, when I was trying to make sense of who I was and why my life felt so off track. This idea is one of the reasons I am writing this book: to nurture your spiritual growth so you can live a spiritually fulfilling life. And when you do, you'll discover that everything you truly need will be provided for you. This is true.

"I closed my eyes and found peace. I looked within, and love poured through. Wings surrounded my heart, and I felt home."
~ Barbara Wainwright

Richard Bach, author of *Illusions: The Adventures of a Reluctant Messiah*, wrote, "We teach best what we most need to learn." That truth resonates with me. The more I teach and give, the more I receive. I believe the same will be true for you. Once you begin to recognize your gifts and take small steps to bring them into the world, you will be rewarded.

Have you ever had an idea for a product, service, or company that felt inspired—and then, not long after, you saw that very thing advertised somewhere else? Here's what I believe: divine inspiration is available to all of us at the same time. But not everyone tunes in to hear the messages, and fewer still take action.

For example, five years ago I heard the clear message that I was meant to create a daily podcast. I resisted at first, but eventually I recorded over sixty episodes of *Show Up for God and God Will Show Up for You in Miraculous Ways*. Later, I was nudged to turn that content into a book—the very one you are holding now. In the process, I rediscovered a document I had written thirteen years earlier that turned out to be exactly what I needed to easily complete this manuscript. God truly does work in miraculous ways—and yes, I have been a reluctant messenger.

Here's the message for you: when you are inspired to do something—when you hear that call from God, the Universe, the Creator (whatever name you use)—know that it's for a reason. The inspiration is meant for you to create and manifest it in the world. Don't worry if others are doing something similar; they will do it their way, and you will do it yours—in your own unique, beautiful, magnificent way.

Keep moving forward. The right doors will open. The right people will appear. The right ideas will be given to you. Continue to listen, continue to act, and continue to trust. Step into your greatness, step into who you are called to be. Start now, and succeed one baby step at a time.

Be the Flame that Lights Others Up

*"The free soul is rare, but you know it when you see it—
basically because you feel good, very good, when you are
near or with them."*

~ Charles Bukowski

Charles Bukowski's words invite us to notice how others make us feel. The presence of a "free soul" is unmistakable: their energy uplifts you simply by being near them.

I encourage you to reflect on this each time you interact with someone—even in ordinary places, like standing in line at the grocery store. A smile or an encouraging word has the power to change someone's day, or even their life. Sometimes all it takes is a small act of kindness to lift someone from a rough moment or to ease their challenges.

Too often, I notice people walking with their heads down, disconnected from the present moment. When we are fully present, we are lit up—aware of the trees, the breeze moving through the leaves, and the simple beauty of life unfolding around us. If you encounter someone who looks discouraged, a kind word or gesture can help draw them back to presence. That, in itself, is a profound gift—perhaps even your unique way of contributing to the world.

Maybe your gift is helping others return to the present so they can fully enjoy their lives. When you yourself are present, you allow love energy to flow through you, enriching your own experience while creating space to share it with others.

Accept it, receive it, and then extend it—especially to those who need it most in that moment.

Each time you help someone heal or navigate a challenge, you are channeling love and healing energy through yourself. And here's the miracle: in blessing others, you are blessed in return. By lifting people into presence, you not only transform their experience—you deepen your own.

Receiving Is Giving

"Give whatever you are doing and whoever you are with the gift of your attention."

~ Jim Rohn

Be generous with your time. The greatest gift we can give another person is our full attention—our presence. Time is our most limited resource, and only God knows how much of it we truly have left.

That said, it's equally important to remain open to receiving as much as we give. Life is a balance of giving and receiving. Many people are naturally warmhearted, compassionate, loving, and generous. Yet givers often struggle to receive. Is that you?

If so, consider this: givers must also open the part of themselves that says, *I am willing to be blessed. I welcome the gifts others want to share with me.*

Receiving creates an exchange of energy. Think about how good it feels when you give—when you brighten someone's day, bring them joy, or show up with a thoughtful gesture. That sense of fulfillment is a gift in itself. In the same way, when you allow yourself to receive, you give someone else the opportunity to feel that same joy.

The *yummy* feeling you experience when giving is the very feeling you gift to another when you graciously receive. By opening yourself to others' generosity, you allow them to experience the blessing of giving back.

So be open to receive. Accept the gifts others wish to share with you. In doing so, you're not just receiving—you're also giving them the profound gift of giving, which is in itself deeply fulfilling.

Your Calling Is Within

"Look to what you have around you and be grateful instead of searching for more. All you can take with you when you leave this world is love, friendship, and good deeds."

~ Sylvia Brown

Many people become consumed with collecting things. Some acquire so much that they must move into bigger spaces simply to store it all. Others are so identified with their possessions that losing them would leave them feeling lost, empty, or broken. Often we display our things to prove our worth: "Come see my new car, my new house, my new outfit."

But is that really what life is about?

Pause a moment to contemplate: Is it more important to accumulate possessions, or to cultivate meaningful relationships? To live with compassion, or to own more things? To feel fulfilled from the inside out, or to rely on outside objects to create fleeting satisfaction? Wouldn't you rather feel good about how you've treated people, contributed to the world, and given of yourself—rather than tallying what you've received? And while receiving is certainly important, isn't giving equally so?

Possessions don't make you a good person. They don't define who you are. Inner fulfillment comes from discovering your true self. This requires stillness—taking a deep breath, quieting your mind, and asking your higher self, *"What is within me that I am meant to share with the world?"* When the answer comes, don't dismiss it. That is your truth. Resist the urge to shrink back. Your Higher Self would not have revealed it unless you were meant to act on it. This is where trust comes in. Trust your inner voice.

> *"You are here to enable the Divine Purpose of the Universe to unfold. That is how important you are."*
> —*Eckhart Tolle*

I believe this is true for every human being. Each of us incarnated into this lifetime with a purpose. You may not know it right away. It often takes exploration—trying, failing, and discovering what truly resonates as your truth. You might begin by asking, *"What can I do that will make the world better for all people?"*

Maybe you're a teacher, shaping young minds—a tremendous gift to humanity. Perhaps you love to cook, creating nourishing meals that bring joy and health to others. You may be a physician, devoted to healing. Whatever your calling, you are meant to shine your light and share your beloved, sacred creation for the betterment of the world.

I encourage you to discover your higher calling and begin taking steps toward it. If you don't yet know what it is, seek guidance from a life coach or someone skilled in asking the right questions. No one can tell you your purpose—it must come from within. Get quiet. Listen deeply. Ask your Higher Self, *"What am I called to do? What is within me that longs to be expressed in the world?"*

Divine Gifts Are Within All of Us

"Your purpose in life is to find your purpose and give your whole heart and soul to it"

~ Buddha

"The meaning of life is to find your gift. The purpose of life is to give it away."

~ Pablo Picasso

"Show up for God so that God will show up for you in miraculous ways."

This message has been in my heart for a long time. I have felt called to share how vital it is to express the divine gifts you were born with. We all come into this world with unique gifts meant to be given back. *What are yours? What are you being called to share?*

Buddha said, "Your purpose in life is to find your purpose and give your whole heart and soul to it." I believe there is even more to it than that. Discovering your purpose means recognizing the divine gifts within you—acknowledging, trusting, and embracing them. Everyone is born with a divine gift, a purpose meant to serve others. Once you discover yours, the next step is to take action. Embody it. Share it. Turn toward the world and give your gift back.

Picasso echoed this truth: "The meaning of life is to find your gift. The purpose of life is to give it away." I believe this wholeheartedly. For years, I felt called to write these words: *"Show up for God, and God will show up for you in miraculous ways."* Yet I procrastinated. I delayed. I avoided taking action.

That changed when I was teaching my Certified Professional Coaching class. One of my students—already a certified coach—challenged me to stop waiting and begin. Another offered to be my accountability partner. That was the moment I knew it was time to show up. So here I am—keeping my commitment, honoring the call in my heart, and sharing this message with you.

Now I am asking you to do the same. Take your divine gift and offer it back to the world. Only you know what that gift is. Only you can choose to express it. Start small if you need to. Take one step a day. Even baby steps move you forward. That is how I have come this far—one small, consistent step at a time.

So today, I invite you: take that next step. Share your gift. Give back to the world what God has placed within you.

Growth Rarely Happens in Our Comfort Zone

"Expectations are resentments waiting to happen."
~ Anne Lamott

Anne Lamott's words remind us of the quiet disappointment that follows when we rely on others to fulfill their promises, only to be let down. When expectations go unmet, resentment can quietly take root.

"Don't join an easy crowd; you won't grow.
Go where the expectations and the demands to perform are
high."
~ Jim Rohn

Jim Rohn offers a different perspective. His words encourage us to lean into challenges and place ourselves in environments that stretch us and call us higher. Growth rarely happens in our comfort zone. By choosing higher standards—and rising to meet them—we strengthen our character. It is a mindset shift that aligns beautifully with our commitment to showing up for God in extraordinary ways.

"There are only two ways to live your life. One is as though
nothing is a miracle. The other is as though everything is a
miracle."
— Albert Einstein

Albert Einstein brings these ideas full circle. What a profound shift in perspective. When we choose to see life as a continuous unfolding of miracles, our outlook changes. As you follow your heart and intuition, you begin to witness blessings that accompany living in alignment with your divine calling.

I encourage you to stay the course on the path where you feel nudged. Each step you take toward sharing your gifts and honoring your calling is not only a testament to your commitment, but also a magnet for miracles. By shining your light and leading by example, you invite others to do the same. And as you continue to show up for God, prepare to be amazed by the miraculous moments that will unfold in your life.

Boldness Has Genius, Power and Magic in It

"There is no passion to be found playing small—in settling for a life that is less than the one you are capable of living."
~ Nelson Mandela

"Whatever you can do, or dream you can, begin it. Boldness has genius, power, and magic in it."
~ W. H. Murray

I believe we are all meant to share our gifts with the world, and in writing this book, I am practicing what I preach. To be honest, I was hesitant—nervous, even scared. I resisted at first, yet the nudges kept coming. I knew I was being guided.

I also believe we are rewarded when we take small steps and follow our intuition, our inner guidance. Each time I've taken a step forward, opportunities to stretch and grow have opened before me. It can feel scary—the fear of the unknown is real— but I continue to move forward because I trust the Universe to provide exactly what I need, in divine and perfect timing.

Perhaps you've had this thought: *I know I should be doing this thing, but I'm not—and I don't feel good about it.* If so, I can relate. My encouragement to you is this: feel the fear and move forward anyway. Fear may always be there—the fear of not knowing what comes next, of investing time, energy, or resources without certainty of the outcome. In truth, what you are really investing in is yourself. You are investing in the adventure, in the pursuit of the calling that won't leave

you alone. Deep down, you know the path is right because you've checked in with your higher guidance, your intuition. You've watched for the signs, and you've received confirmation.

This is how the Universe works. Take those baby steps and go for it. Since beginning the steps toward the manifestation of this book, I've been presented with opportunities I never could have imagined. Be brave. Be bold. Do what you are being called to do. Feel the fear—and do it anyway.

And if you feel stuck, not knowing what the next step should be, take some quiet time. Meditate. Ask your inner guidance: *What is the next best step for me to take?* The answer will come—perhaps in unexpected ways, but it will come. The most important thing is to keep moving forward, one step at a time. Doors will open, and your dream will begin to manifest.

Show up for God, and God will show up for you in miraculous ways.

Show Up for God and God will Show Up for You in Miraculous Ways

Afterword

The Power of the Subconscious Mind

"Whatever we plant in our subconscious mind and nourish with repetition and emotion will one day become a reality."
~ Earl Nightingale

Through my coaching system, I have seen this truth in action. We teach our coaches how to help clients reprogram their subconscious minds with thoughts that truly nourish them. When this happens, the client's mind, body, and spirit are infused with energy and emotion, because the new program reflects what they have often been dreaming of for years—sometimes even decades.

"The subconscious mind is more susceptible to influence by impulses of thought mixed with 'feeling' or emotion than by those originating solely in the reasoning portion of the mind."
~ Napoleon Hill

This is why affirmations don't always work. Affirmations often come from the reasoning, logical mind: *I'm rich, rich, rich* or *I now have abundance flowing through me.* These are powerful statements, but if they aren't infused with genuine emotion and feeling, then—just as Hill described—you're unlikely to see results.

In our coaching classes, we share a process that helps clients uncover what truly drives them—what lights them up, what they long to create, and what will bring fulfillment and impact to their own lives and to the lives of others. What gift do you have to give back to the world? And what excuse, fear, or obstacle is still standing in your way? It's time to face it, rise above it, and step fully into the life you are meant to create.

I encourage you to dream big. What is in your heart to create and share? Once you see it clearly, begin taking small, steady steps toward making it real. Sometimes, though, we don't realize what is hidden in our subconscious minds. The subconscious is largely programmed from birth to about age eight, and most of us don't remember much from those years. That is why so many of us carry limiting beliefs we're not even aware of—beliefs that quietly hold us back.

This is why we guide clients to uncover what their hearts truly want to create. From there, we help them shape their vision into a statement that can reprogram the subconscious mind. When clients listen to that vision repeatedly, the combination of repetition and genuine emotion fuels their excitement—and that's when manifestation accelerates. Breakthroughs come faster than they ever imagined.

It is incredibly rewarding to witness. As a coach, there is nothing quite like watching a client break free and light up as their body, mind, and spirit shift into alignment with their true purpose.

Breaking Free of Your Comfort Zone

"Challenge yourself; it's the only path which leads to growth."

~ Morgan Freeman

"If you're unwilling to leave someplace you've outgrown, you will never reach your full potential. To be the best, you have to constantly be challenging yourself, raising the bar, pushing the limits of what you can do. Don't stand still, leap forward."

~ Ronda Rousey

Stepping outside your comfort zone can feel daunting. It stirs up stress, anxiety, and the temptation to remain within the familiar. The subconscious mind—designed to keep us safe—often reacts with resistance. This resistance can appear as self-sabotage, a fight-or-flight response, or a general sense of unease. Yet comfort zones, while safe, are also limiting.

Morgan Freeman's words cut to the truth: growth begins only when we dare to challenge ourselves. Every step into the unknown becomes an invitation to expand who we are and what we are capable of. Ronda Rousey echoes this call, reminding us that clinging to what no longer serves us stifles our potential. To reach new heights, we must continuously challenge ourselves by raising the bar, pushing our limits, and leaping forward—even when the path feels uncertain.

In my coaching work, I emphasize a similar philosophy. Each of us carries unique gifts meant to be shared with the world. But stepping into that creative expression requires courage and a willingness to break free from the comfort of the familiar. One of the tools I teach is the creation of a personal vision statement, delivered to every client. This vision statement encompasses their dreams and aspirations and is written as though they have already achieved success.

When clients listen to their vision statement, it reprograms the subconscious mind. They begin to see themselves as successful—living their purpose as a present reality. This alignment between the subconscious and conscious mind gradually dissolves fear and replaces hesitation with confidence. What once felt like a leap becomes not only possible but natural. Seeing their success in the mind's eye, over and over, allows them to step forward with calm assurance, free from the anxiety and stress of change.

If you find yourself standing on the edge of that first step—whether small or monumental—know this: you don't have to take it alone. Support is available, whether through coaching or self-guided practices. What matters most is that you begin. Your comfort zone may feel safe, but your growth lies beyond it. Dare to step forward, and you will discover not only who you are, but who you were always meant to become.

The Power of Life Coaching

"10% of what we read, we learn; we learn 20% of what we hear; 30% of what we see; 50% of what we both hear and see; 70% of what is discussed; 80% of what we experience personally, and 95% of what we teach to someone else."

~ William Glasser

In our life coach training and certification course, you will experience personally what we teach. You will receive coaching, your vision statement, and identify the steps to get started on your path. You will also coach someone, write their vision statement and coach them to identify the next best steps they need to take.

"Knowing is not enough; we must apply. Willing is not enough; we must do."

~ Johann Wolfgang von Goethe

This truth is evident in our course. You will not only learn what to do but also practice and apply what you learn. You will experience receiving coaching as a client and applying the coaching methods as a coach. You will be fully immersed in the world of coaching while learning the Wainwright Method of Coaching.

"In a time of drastic change, which, if you take a look around, we're definitely in a time of drastic change, it is the learners who inherit the future."

~ Eric Hoffer

When you learn to serve others and help them transform through our proven coaching system, you gain the joy of witnessing their breakthroughs. It is deeply fulfilling to watch clients light up with their aha moment—when they finally say, "This is what I have been dreaming of, hoping for, wishing for so long. Now I feel confident that I can do it. I can see myself being successful and know it will become my truth." That is the reward.

I invite you to join our coaching class. It is sixteen hours long—fun, fast, affordable, and joyful. Best of all, you'll meet other people on the same path, ready to change the world for the better, one client at a time.

The Wainwright Global Coaching Course equips students with techniques to heighten consciousness, strengthen awareness, and align with their Divine Purpose. If you feel called to become a certified professional coach, this training can benefit not only you but also every client you serve. The practices you learn will help you navigate life with clarity, presence, and intention.

Book Quote References

References (Alphabetical by Author Last Name)

All quotes accessed October 10, 2025 on
https://www.brainyquote.com/quotes/

Abilene, Laura. "Nothing is about finding anything outside of ourselves; everything is about becoming that which we seek. Don't look for love; become love. Don't look for happiness; be happy. Don't look for kindness; be kind. Don't look for change; become the change. Life is an inside job; our soul has the answers."

Angelou, Maya. "I've learned that people will forget what you said, people will forget what you did, but people will never forget how you made them feel."

Anthony, Robert. "Your conscious desires and your subconscious intention must be in alignment. If your conscious mind wants one thing and the subconscious mind wants something else, it's impossible to create what you truly want."

Aquinas, Thomas. "Man cannot live without joy; therefore when he is deprived of true spiritual joys it is necessary that he become addicted to carnal pleasures."

Bach, Richard. "You are never given a dream without also being given the power to make it come true. You may have to work for it, however."

Bach, Richard. "Don't believe what your eyes are telling you. All they show is limitation. Look with your understanding. Find out what you already know and you will see the way to fly."

Bradford, John. "There but for the grace of God go I."

Branson, Richard. "Learn to use your brainpower; critical thinking is the key to creative problem-solving in business."

Brown, Eleanor. "Some people are going to love you no matter what you do, and some people will never love you no matter what you do. Go where the love is."

Brown, Eleanor. "There are times in our lives when we have to realize our past is precisely what it is, and we cannot change it, but we can change the story we tell ourselves about it, and by doing that, we can change the future."

Brown, Les. "Change your thinking, change your life. Your thoughts create your reality. Practice positive thinking, act the way you want to be, and soon you will be the way you act."

Browne, Sylvia. "Look to what you have around you and be grateful instead of searching for more. All you can take with you when you leave this world is love, friendship, and good deeds."

Bukowski, Charles. "The free soul is rare, but you know it when you see it - basically because you feel good, very good, when you are near or with them."

Bryan, William Jennings. "Destiny is not a matter of chance. It is a matter of choice. It is not a thing to be waited for, it is a thing to be achieved."

Buddha. "Your purpose in life is to find your purpose and give your whole heart and soul to it."

Canfield, Jack. "Change is inevitable in life. You can either resist it and potentially get run over by it, or you can choose to cooperate with it, adapt to it, and learn how to benefit from it. When you embrace change you will begin to see it as an opportunity for growth."

Carnegie, Dale. "Our fatigue is often caused not by work but by worry, frustration, and resentment."

Cattrall, Kim. "I try not to listen to the shoulds or coulds, and try to get beyond expectations, peer pressure, or trying to please - and just listen. I believe all the answers are ultimately within us."

Chopra, Deepak. "In a quiet place, close your eyes, take a deep breath, and go inward. Place your attention on your heart, in the center of your chest. Sit quietly and easily let your attention remain there."

Chopra, Deepak. "When you live your life with an appreciation of coincidences and their meanings, you connect with the underlying field of infinite possibilities."

Coelho, Paulo. "When you want something; all the universe conspires in helping you to achieve it."

Collier, Robert. "Our subconscious minds have no sense of humor, play no jokes and cannot tell the difference between reality and an imagined thought or image. What we continually think about eventually will manifest in our lives."

Crippen, Craig. "As you awaken, you will come to understand that the journey to love is about becoming the one, not finding the one."

Dana, Deb. "Have you heard about glimmers? They are the opposite of triggers. A glimmer is a tiny micro moment of happiness, a sign of hope. Once you begin to look for them, they will start to appear everywhere."

Dali, Salvador. "Have no fear of perfection - you'll never reach it."

Dyer, Wayne, "With God, all things are possible."

Einstein, Albert. "Anyone who doesn't take truth seriously in small matters cannot be trusted in large ones either."

Einstein, Albert. "There are only two ways to live your life. One is as though nothing is a miracle. The other is as though everything is a miracle."

Einstein, Albert. "We cannot solve our problems with the same thinking we used when we created them."

Eliot, John. "Thinking is a habit, and like any other habit, it can be changed; it just takes effort and repetition."

Feldt, Gloria. "Embrace controversy. It gives you a platform. It is a teacher, a clarifier, and your friend, especially if you are trying to make a change."

Ford, Henry. "Most people spend more time and energy going around problems than in trying to solve them."

Freeman, Morgan. "Challenge yourself; it's the only path which leads to growth."

Gibran, Khalil. "When you are sorrowful, look again in your heart, and you shall see that in truth you are weeping for that which has been your delight."

Glasser, William. "10% of what we read, we learn; we learn 20% of what we hear; 30% of what we see; 50% of what we both hear and see; 70% of what is discussed; 80% of what we experience personally, and 95% of what we teach to someone else."

Goethe, Johann Wolfgang von. "Knowing is not enough; we must apply. Willing is not enough; we must do."

Graham, Martha. "Some men have thousands of reasons why they cannot do what they want to do when all they need is one reason why they can."

Grover, Tim. "Luck becomes a convenient excuse when things don't go your way, and luck is a rationale for staying comfortable while you wait for luck to determine your fate."

Hendricks, Gay. "The goal in life is not to attain some imaginary ideal; it is to find and fully use our own gifts."

Hendricks, Gay. "The main reason intuition is so important is this: It's a clear sign that you're connecting with your inner spiritual guidance system. Intuition is a direct signal from your deepest self that you are navigating from your true center."

Hendricks, Gay. "You never know when it is going to happen, when you will experience a moment that dramatically transforms your life. When you look back, often years later, you may see how a brief conversation or an insight you read somewhere, changed the entire course of your life."

Hiddleston, Tom. "Stay hungry, stay young, stay foolish, stay curious, and above all, stay humble because just when you think you got all the answers, is the moment when some bitter twist of fate in the universe will remind you that you very much don't."

Hill, Napoleon. "Self-discipline begins with the mastery of your thoughts. If you don't control what you think, you can't control what you do. Simply, self-discipline enables you to think first and act afterward."

Hill, Napoleon. "Indecision, doubt, and fear—the members of this Unholy Trio—are closely related. Where one is found, the other two are close at hand."

Hill, Napoleon. "The subconscious mind is more susceptible to influence by impulses of thought mixed with 'feeling' or emotion, than by those originating solely in the reasoning portion of the mind."

Holmes, Lewis. "I believe you are robbing the world of who you are when you have a gift to share with others but let fear hold you back from expressing it."

Hoffer, Eric. "In a time of drastic change, which, if you take a look around, we're definitely in a time of drastic change, it is the learners who inherit the future."

Isaacson, Walter. "Here's to the crazy ones. The misfits. The rebels. The troublemakers. The round pegs in the square holes. The ones who see things differently."

Jackson, Michael. "I'm never pleased with anything, I'm a perfectionist, it's part of who I am."

Jung Carl. "Even a happy life cannot be without a measure of darkness, and the word happy would lose its meaning if it were not balanced by sadness."

Katie, Byron. "Life is simple. Everything happens for you, not to you. Everything happens at exactly the right moment, neither too soon nor too late. You don't have to like it... it's just easier if you do."

King, Martin Luther Jr. "The ultimate measure of a man is not where he stands in moments of comfort and convenience, but where he stands at times of challenge and controversy."

Lamott, Anne. "Expectations are resentments waiting to happen."

Lenz, Frederick. "As you evolve and develop your psychic abilities, you will enter into perceptions of life, truth, beauty and you will gain power to live your life in an intelligent, perceptive and strong way."

Lessin, Roy. "God is bigger than time, dates, and appointments. He wants you to move through this day with a quiet heart, an inward assurance that He is in control, a peaceful certainty that your life is in His hands, a deep trust in His plan and purposes, and a thankful disposition toward all that He allows. He wants you to put your faith in Him, not in a timetable. He wants you to wait on Him and wait for Him. In his perfect way, He will put everything together, see to every detail, arrange every circumstance, and order every step to bring to pass what He has for you.'"

Lincoln, Abraham. "Commitment is what transforms a promise into a reality... Commitment is the stuff character is made of; the power to change the face of things. It is the daily triumph of integrity over skepticism."

Lipton, Bruce. "People need to realize that their thoughts are more primary than their genes, because the environment, which is influenced by our thoughts, controls the genes."

Lipton, Bruce. "Change your thoughts through repetition and the creation of 'habits,' which is the primary way we acquire subconscious programs after age 7. This can't just be sticky notes on the mirror. This must be felt and experienced."

Lucado, Max. "You weren't an accident; you weren't mass-produced. You aren't an assembly-line product; you were deliberately planned, so specifically gifted and lovingly positioned on the Earth by the master Craftsman."

Loder, Ted. "Laughter is a holy thing. It is as sacred as music and silence and solemnity, maybe more sacred. Laughter is like a prayer, like a bridge over which creatures tiptoe to meet each other. Laughter is like mercy; it heals. When you can laugh at yourself, you are free."

Lombardi, Vince. "Perfection is not attainable, but if we chase perfection we can catch excellence."

Mandela, Nelson. "I learned that courage was not the absence of fear, but the triumph over it. The brave man is not the one who does not feel afraid, but he who conquers that fear."

Mandela, Nelson. "Resentment is like drinking poison and then hoping it will kill your enemies."

Mandela, Nelson. "There is no passion to be found playing small - in settling for a life that is less than the one you are capable of living."

Maxwell, John C. "Motivation gets you going, but discipline keeps you growing. That's the Law of consistency. It doesn't matter how talented you are; it doesn't matter how many opportunities you receive. If you want to grow, consistency is the key. Small disciplines repeated with consistency every day lead to great achievements gained slowly over time."

McKay, Harvey. "Fatigue makes fools of us all; it robs us of our skill, our judgment, and blinds us to creative solutions."

Moen, Don. "God will make a way where there seems to be no way. He works in ways that we cannot see."

Murray, W. H. "Whatever you can do, or dream you can, begin it. Boldness has genius, power and magic in it."

Myss, Caroline. "Facing personal truths and purging yourself of addictions or manipulative habits require strength, courage, humility, faith, and other qualities of a soul with stamina, because you are not just changing yourself; you are changing your universe. Your soul is a compass. Change one coordinate in your spiritual compass and you change your entire life's direction."

Nelson, Barbara M. "We are all born with divine gifts that we are meant to share with the world. Shine your light and lead the way for others."

Niebuhr, Reinhold. "God, grant me the serenity to accept the things I cannot change, the courage to change the things I can, and the wisdom to know the difference."

Nightingale, Earl. "Whatever we plant in our subconscious mind and nourish with repetition and emotion will one day become a reality."

Nouwen, Henry. "Compassion asks us to go where it hurts, to enter into faces of pain, to share in brokenness, fear, confusion, and anguish. Compassion challenges us to cry out with those in misery, to mourn with those who are lonely, to weep with those in tears. Compassion requires us to be weak with the weak, vulnerable with the vulnerable, and powerless with the powerless. Compassion means full immersion into the condition of being human."

Olson, Jeff. "Showing up is essential. Showing up consistently is powerful. Showing up consistently with a positive outlook is even more powerful."

Oxford English Dictionary. "Divine Grace is the Divine influence that operates in humans to regenerate and sanctify, to inspire virtuous impulses, and to impart strength to endure trials and resist temptation."

Peck, M. Scott. "When I genuinely love I am extending myself, and when I am extending myself I am growing. The more I love, the longer I love, the larger I become. Genuine love is self-replenishing. The more I nurture the spiritual growth of others, the more my own spiritual growth is nurtured."

Picasso, Pablo. "The meaning of life is to find your gift. The purpose of life is to give it away."

Ponder, Catherine. "When you hold resentment toward another, you are bound to that person or condition by an emotional link that is stronger than steel. Forgiveness is the only way to dissolve that link and get free."

Roberts, Jane. "You are so part of the world that your slightest action contributes to its reality. Your breath changes the atmosphere. Your encounters with others alter the fabrics of their lives, and the lives of those who come in contact with them."

Rohn, Jim. "Don't join an easy crowd; you won't grow. Go where the expectations and the demands to perform are high."

Rohn, Jim. "Give whatever you are doing and whoever you are with the gift of your attention."

Rousey, Ronda. "If you're unwilling to leave someplace you've outgrown, you will never reach your full potential. To be the best, you have to constantly be challenging yourself, raising the bar, pushing the limits of what you can do. Don't stand still, leap forward."

Schweitzer, Albert. "Success is not the key to happiness. Happiness is the key to success. If you love what you are doing, you will be successful."

Seuss, Dr. "Don't cry because it's over. Smile because it happened."

Sheen, Fulton J. "Patience is power. Patience is not an absence of action; rather it is 'timing'. It waits on the right time to act, for the right principles and in the right way."

Stamp, Josiah. "It's easy to dodge our responsibilities, but we cannot dodge the consequences of dodging our responsibilities."

Tolle, Eckhart. "A deep-seated state of fear, need, lack, and incompleteness is part of the human condition in its unredeemed and unenlightened state. In an enlightened state, the individual possesses a profound clarity of vision and understanding, allowing them to navigate life's complexities with heightened awareness."

Tolle, Eckhart. "Every addiction arises from an unconscious refusal to face and move through your own pain. Every addiction starts with pain and ends with pain. Whatever the substance you are addicted to - alcohol, food, legal or illegal drugs, or a person - you are using something or somebody to cover up your pain."

Tolle, Eckhart. "Most of the so-called bad things that happen in people's lives are due to unconsciousness. They are self-created, or rather, ego-created dramas. When you are fully conscious, drama does not come into your life anymore."

Tolle, Eckhart. "Is suffering really necessary? Yes and no. If you had not suffered as you have, there would be no depth to you, no humility, and no compassion. Suffering cracks open the shell of ego, and then comes a point when it has served its purpose. Suffering is necessary until you realize it is unnecessary. True freedom and the end of suffering are living in such a way as if you had completely chosen whatever you feel or experience at this moment. This inner alignment with now is the end of suffering."

Tolle, Eckhart. "You are here to enable the Divine Purpose of the universe to unfold. That is how important you are."

Unknown, Author. "As you evolve you will make a lot of people uncomfortable. Evolve anyway."

Wainwright, Barbara. "After witnessing miracles over a period of time, you begin to believe in them."

Wainwright, Barbara. "God, grant me serenity as I open to receive abundantly. Grace me with the courage and inner strength to ask for more and to receive more. Bless me with Your Divine Wisdom to know I am worthy and loved. For who am I to judge my value, and who am I to judge the value I am destined to bring to the world?"

Wainwright, Barbara. "I closed my eyes and found peace. I looked within and love poured through. Wings surrounded my heart and I felt home."

Wainwright, Barbara. "We are all born with divine gifts that we are meant to share with the world. Shine your light and lead the way for others."

Walsch, Neale Donald. "Don't dismiss the synchronicity of what is happening right now finding its way into your life at just this moment. There are no coincidences in the universe, only convergences of will, intent, and experience."

White, Barbara M. "Building trust is a process. Trust results from consistent and predictable interaction over time."

Welling, Tom. "I have so much chaos in my life, it's become normal. You become used to it. You have to just relax, calm down, take a deep breath and try to see how you can make things work rather than complain about how they're wrong."

Ziglar, Zig. "Honesty and integrity are absolutely essential for success in all areas of life. The really good news is that anyone can develop both honesty and integrity."

About the Author

Barbara G. Wainwright, Certified Master Life Coach and CEO of Wainwright Global, is recognized as one of the most sought-after teachers in the coaching and self-empowerment industry. Since 2006, she has trained and certified more than 6,600 professional coaches worldwide and developed the acclaimed *Wainwright Method of Coaching*, empowering individuals to actualize their life purpose, live inspired lives, and connect with their true passion.

Her corporate clients have included Boeing, Syracuse University, and Washington University, among others. An international speaker, author, and educator, Barbara has published five books available on Amazon and co-hosts the popular podcast *The Power of Now: A Guide to Spiritual Enlightenment with Gilda and Barbara*, which has surpassed one million downloads. She has also produced over 65 video shorts in her series *Show Up for God and God Will Show Up for You in Miraculous Ways*.

Barbara's free guide, *10 Essential Things You Absolutely Must Know Before You Start Your Coaching Career*, is available at WainwrightGlobal.com. When she isn't serving clients and students around the world, Barbara enjoys spending time with family and her grandson and embracing the beauty of Newport Beach, California, where she resides.

Barbara G. Wainwright, CPC
Available for Services

Barbara is available for speaking engagements, podcasts, and Life Coach Training & Certification.

Barbara can be reached at:
949-281-6737 and Barbara@WainwrightGlobal.com

For more information, visit her website:
https://www.WainwrightGlobal.com

You can access her website via this QR code.

Other Works by Barbara G. Wainwright

Books Available on Amazon.com

The Power of Life Coaching Volume 4: Manifesting Transformation in Financial, Professional, Emotional, Spiritual, Wellness and Relationship Aspects

The Power of Life Coaching Volume 3: Manifesting Transformation in Financial, Professional, Emotional, Spiritual, Wellness and Relationship Aspects

The Power of Life Coaching Volume 2: Manifesting Transformation in Financial, Professional, Emotional, Spiritual, Wellness and Relationship Aspects

The Power of Coaching: Manifesting Transformation in the World

Books Available on WainwrightGlobal.com

10 Essential Things You Absolutely Must Know Before You Start Your Coaching Career

52 Life Coaching Niches Working Miracles Every Day

Awakening to Divine Purpose: The Six Stages of Spiritual Transformation

Podcast Available on Spotify.com

The Power of Now - A Spiritual Guide to Enlightenment
with Gilda and Barbara

Video Shorts Available on Youtube.com

Show Up for God and God Will Show Up for You in
Miraculous Ways

Streaming Radio Available on KPHRED.com

KPRHED Prime Live – Studio Audience Event

Available on Authority Magazine

Barbara Wainwright: Five Things You Need to Create a
Highly Successful Career as a Life or Business Coach

Available on Disrupt Magazine

Barbara Wainwright: Pioneering Change Through Coaching
and Self-Direction

Available on NY Weekly

Embrace Your Encore: Retirees Redefining Retirement
Through Coaching

New Book Coming Soon

Angelic Conversations: Embodying Your Spiritual Calling

Notes

Notes